PARENT, TEACHER, MENTOR, FRIEND

How **every adult**
can change kids' lives

Peter L. Benson, Ph.D.

SEARCH
INSTITUTE
PRESS

To the Mentors of
Mankato YMCA —
Keep up the
great work.
Pete Ben —

PARENT, TEACHER, MENTOR, FRIEND
How Every Adult Can Change Kids' Lives
Peter L. Benson, Ph.D.
The following are registered trademarks of Search Institute:
Search Institute®, Developmental Assets®, and Healthy
Communities • Healthy Youth®.

10 9 8 7 6 5 4 3 2 1
Printed on acid-free paper in the United States of America.

Search Institute
615 First Avenue Northeast, Suite 125
Minneapolis, MN 55413
www.search-institute.org
612-376-8955 • 877-240-7251, ext. 1

ISBN-13: 978-1-57482-283-0

Credits
Editor: Tenessa Gemelke
Book Design: Jeenee Lee
Production Supervisor: Mary Ellen Buscher

Library of Congress Cataloging-in-Publication Data
Benson, Peter L.
Parent, teacher, mentor, friend : how every adult can change
kids' lives / Peter L. Benson.
    p. cm.
    Includes bibliographical references.
    ISBN-13: 978-1-57482-283-0 (pbk. : alk. paper)
    ISBN-10: 1-57482-283-7 (pbk. : alk. paper)
    1. Child development. 2. Children and adults.
3. Children—Counseling of. 4. Teenagers—Counseling of.
5. Parenting. 6. Mentoring. I. Title.
HQ767.9.B435 2010
649'.6—dc22
                                    2010035775

To Barbara Varenhorst,
lifelong friend to children everywhere

CONTENTS

A Call to Action

*One hundred years from now it will not matter
what kind of car I drove, what kind of house I
lived in, how much money I had in my bank
account, or what my clothes looked like. But one
hundred years from now the world may be a
little better because I was important in the life of
a child.* ANONYMOUS

These words are powerful. Here is one
of life's ultimate truths—a maxim that
gets too easily lost in the speed and
intensity of our lives. The wisdom is time-
less, of course. And every generation needs
to hear it, over and over again. Five hundred years ago, German theologian Martin
Luther observed, "Indeed, for what purpose

do we older folks exist, other than to care for, instruct, and bring up the young?" This is a charge he gave not just to parents but, in his words, "to every citizen."

Every citizen. That means you. That means me. And everyone we hang out with—at work, in our neighborhoods, online—within whatever networks we operate. Whether we are old or young, male or female, rich or poor, we are all responsible for the children our culture is raising.

What Can We Do?

You are probably reading this book because you care deeply about kids. Perhaps you see kids struggling in the course of your work, in your family, or in your neighborhood. Or maybe you know kids who are "just getting by," but they aren't fully engaged with the world around them. You have a sense that you should be *doing* something, but you're not sure what.

Ernie Cortes is one of America's premier community builders. He does this for a living. He reminds us that "we know it takes a village to raise a child . . . but do we now know how to build a village?"

This society of ours is not centered on young people. This is particularly true for teenagers. In this delicate stage of life, it is common for an adolescent to feel disconnected from all adults (perhaps even those in her or his own family), to be a stranger in her or his neighborhood, to be ignored or unwelcome in public places, to be the reluctant target of well-intentioned programs (without any say in their focus or design), and to spend considerable time each day without any adult presence. Teens may give the impression that they prefer this solitude, but even when they appear to be moody or withdrawn, research shows that they actually need and appreciate adult attention and affirmation. To leave these young people disconnected and struggling is a tragedy.

That's our charge: to connect each child and teenager with many caring adults who are willing to be sources of support and guidance—from building authentic relationships with them to voting for candidates who support youth-centered policies. When each of us heeds this call to action, we begin to build communities in which young people thrive.

When it comes to raising healthy and whole kids, every community member matters. Even the smallest of actions matters. Think of it this way: raising great kids is so much easier when all adults use their natural abilities to name, know, watch out for, cherish, and support young people. Families function better when other adults rally around kids. Schools are more successful when they are embedded in a web of community support. The web is critical and essential. It reminds me of an Ethiopian proverb: "When spider webs unite, they can tie up a lion."

So which threads do you contribute to this web? Are you a parent? Are you working with kids in a school or program? Are you just getting started as a mentor? Are you a concerned community member who is ready to make a difference? Cortes asks if we know how to build a village. To put it more simply, do *you* know how to build a village? Whether you realize it or not, research shows that you are already capable of making a significant contribution.

> **When spider webs unite, they can tie up a lion.**

The Importance of Caring Adults: What the Research Says

For several decades, the nonprofit organization I lead, Search Institute, has conducted many significant research studies on children and adolescents. Our focus is on understanding the pathways to a successful and healthy life. This work has involved millions of young people around the world. Our research studies are the "think tank" side of Search Institute, and this work involves a team of social scientists who are professionally (and personally) dedicated to discovering what kids need to lead healthy, happy lives.

Search Institute recently conducted an international study of youth in eight nations. These are Australia, Cameroon, Canada, India, Thailand, Ukraine, the United Kingdom, and the United States.[1] We wanted to discover whether life goals for youth are similar or dissimilar around the world. It turns out the world's youth have a lot in common. We found that in these eight countries, there are five life goals that 80 percent (or more) of youth ages 12 to 25 deem important:

- Being hopeful about the future

- Having a sense that life has meaning and purpose

- Making the world a better place

- Protecting the earth's air, land, and water

- Knowing what is unique and valuable about ourselves.

These findings thrill me. As parents, teachers, mentors, and friends, we have these kinds of aspirations for kids. To know that youth also hold these goals for themselves is, as adolescents of one generation might have said, "way cool." Incidentally, "making lots of money" was pretty far down the list of possible responses.

The fact that youth cherish these ideals should give us hope. The fact that youth often lack the supports and opportunities to achieve these ideals should give us pause.

Earlier I mentioned that the "think tank" is only one side of the work Search Institute does. The other side of our work is organized more like an "action tank," with a team of people passionately dedicated to mobilizing families, schools, neighborhoods, and whole communities to nourish the potential in each and every child. Because research shows that this has more to do with how you and I live our lives than policy, money, or programs, it is essential that we convince every caring adult to step up and take action. That's where you come in.

Developmental Assets: Nutrients for Success

As you ponder the important role you can play for kids, think about the things that matter most. What are the supports and opportunities that propel young people to become compassionate, engaged, purposeful, hopeful, and healthy? Which experiences create a scaffold on which children and teens can build strong lives? What developmental nutrients do young people need?

Search Institute has identified a framework that describes these life nutrients. We call them Developmental Assets, and there are 40 of them. (See appendix A on page 171 for the complete list.) Each of the 40, scientifically speaking, contributes to a full, healthy, and successful life. This may seem like a daunting "to-do" list, but you may find it helpful to think of Developmental Assets as the ingredients needed for a really good holiday dinner: lots of people contribute a little something to make the meal successful.

As you read the rest of this book, I'd like you to think about nine of these Developmental Assets. Over the years Search Institute has surveyed more than three million young people in more than 2,000 places to learn how they experience assets. The percentages below reflect the number of young people who reported experiencing each asset in our most recent data:

- *Family Support:* Family life provides high levels of love and support (68%).

- *Positive Family Communication:* Young person and her or his parent(s) communicate positively and frequently (28%).

- *Other Adult Relationships:* Young person receives support from three or more nonparent adults (43%).

- *Caring Neighborhood:* Young person experiences caring neighbors (37%).

- *Caring School Climate:* School provides a caring, encouraging environment (29%).

- *Parent Involvement in Schooling:* Parent(s) are actively involved in helping young person succeed in school (29%).

- *Community Values Youth:* Young person perceives that adults in the community value youth (22%).

- *Youth as Resources:* Young people are given useful roles in the community (26%).

- *Adult Role Models:* Parent(s) and other adults model positive, responsible behavior (27%).[2]

What's common across these nine assets? Each requires adults to create positive, lasting relationships with young people. I marvel at the opportunities these nine assets give to every adult to matter and to make a difference in every community. Obviously, parents are critical for family assets; just think about the additional impact parents can have by being part of the support system for other people's kids.[3] Teachers are critical not only because they work in schools but also because they are a daily source of caring words and actions. And what about neighbors? Librarians? Aunts and uncles? No one person can do it alone, and every adult has a role to play. In your town and mine, there are thousands of individuals who can change kids' lives.

> **Society does not have a youth problem. It has an adult problem.**

Look at the percentages listed after each of the nine assets. Although family support is relatively strong at 68 percent (with emphasis on the word *relatively,* since this number should ideally be 100%), the other asset percentages are pretty . . . I'm searching for a word here. *Disappointing* seems too soft. *Ugly* seems a little harsh. What would you call it? Whatever we call it, we can say with confidence that society does not have a youth problem. It has an *adult* problem.

Making Time, Taking Time

A few years ago, several caring adults attended a town meeting in a Pennsylvania community. All 3,000 middle school and high school students had recently completed a survey to measure their experience of Developmental Assets, and 2,000 adults had gathered to hear the results of the survey.

As the evening began, the first person to speak was the president of the high school senior class. She was poised, articulate, and direct when she said, "I stand before you today to testify why only 21 percent of the young people in this city have asset number 7 (Community Values Youth). You are proud of how you raised money for a new day-care center. You are proud that our football team made it to state this year. But in our daily lives, you no longer make time or take time. You don't know us, many of you are afraid of us, and when you pass by on streets, you scurry by us. You don't know how to slow down and talk to us, and you are so much more fascinated by our problems than our successes."

Talk about a spellbinding speech. You could hear the proverbial pin drop. "You no longer make time or take time." This was the community's wake-up call—a call to action.

Journalist Patricia Hersch spent several years chronicling the intimate lives of teenagers in the Washington, D.C., area. She similarly describes young people as being bereft of adult contact outside their own families and notes the limited contact they have with adults at school. In her words, "America's adolescents have become strangers. They are a tribe apart, mysterious, vaguely threatening. Somewhere in the transition from twelve to thirteen, our nation's children slip into a netherworld of adolescence that too often becomes a self-fulfilling prophecy of estrangement. The individual child feels lost to a world of teens, viewed mostly in the aggregate, notorious for what they do wrong, judged for their inadequacies, known by labels and statistics that frighten and put off adults."[4]

The good news here is that adults *do* care, and it is possible to change course. That town in Pennsylvania is different now. An awakening occurred—a transformation in adult attitudes and behaviors. Although it does take time to make time, this book stands as proof that even small, brief, inexpensive, nearly effortless acts of caring can have a tremendous payoff.

The Power of Relationships

So what does this all mean in our daily lives? After decades of forming hypotheses, conducting and publishing studies, crafting and rewriting definitions, and analyzing data, Search Institute researchers and practitioners have arrived at a surprisingly simple conclusion: nothing—*nothing*—has more impact in the life of a child than positive relationships. In recent years, a compelling body of literature on youth-adult relationships has emerged. Four scientific findings are particularly critical:

- Young people benefit from having many caring adults in their lives. The more adults, the better.

- Healthy relationships with adults (whether they are neighbors, teachers, coaches, mentors, or employers) create a protective buffer against risk behaviors such as the use of alcohol, tobacco, and illicit drugs.

- Supportive relationships are critical to school success and staying in school.

- Relationships become more powerful the longer they are sustained.[5]

Unfortunately, our society is, in some ways, organized to abruptly terminate young people's relationships with adults: teachers are present in a child's

> **Relationships are the oxygen of human development.**

life for a year or less, coaches and leaders of after-school programs come and go, and geographic mobility leads to fewer friendships with extended family members or neighbors. Indeed, it may be getting harder and harder to guarantee that all kids are connected to sustainable relationships.

Relationships are the oxygen of human development. For it is in the embrace of relationships that kids discover their worth, their purpose, their importance in our world. In her novel *Beloved,* Toni Morrison beautifully captures how a supportive adult matters:

"She gathers me. The pieces that I am, she gathers them and gives them back to me in all the right order."

Parents, teachers, mentors, caring adults—what an opportunity we have.

Start Where You Are

Whether you know it or not, you already have tremendous power to change a young person's life. Sometimes adults don't believe their efforts make a difference. One of the best ways to discover what you have to offer is to think back on your own experiences. Who is someone (a parent, teacher, coach, religious leader, neighbor) who . . .

- Helped you realize you had something important to contribute to others?

- Helped you get excited about learning new things?

- Encouraged you to live out positive values, such as caring, honesty, and responsibility?

- Helped you develop important relationship skills and learn how to get along with other people?

- Believed in you and your potential?

- Helped you feel good about yourself and optimistic about your future?

These people may loom large in your memory, but think about the words they said to you. Consider their actions. Did they sit you down and say, "I have vast wisdom to impart, and I am about to change your life"? Probably not. In fact, these adults may have no idea that they left any impression on you at all.

The truth is that most children and teenagers are transformed by the everyday, routine things adults do. These gestures seem like "no big deal." But while the little things may not seem that important or life-changing, small actions and simple words can make all the difference in the world.

> **Small actions and simple words can make all the difference in the world.**

The following five chapters serve as a reminder to all of us of the small, medium, and large ways we can build the web of support for kids. Each chapter provides real-life examples and ideas for action, giving you concrete opportunities to make a difference. The first three chapters are personal:

In 30 Seconds or Less
Make the most of brief interactions with youth.

Connect
Begin to build transformative relationships.

Stay in Touch and Make It Last
Let a young person know that your support is unconditional and unending.

The last two chapters take these ideas even further, suggesting ways you can unite with other adults to make a greater difference:

Stand Up, Act Up
Be an advocate not only for the young people in your life but also for those in your neighborhood, city, or nation.

Start Something
Create a program, initiative, or other opportunity for young people.

I like to think of these efforts as five related rings of action; although some efforts may seem smaller or briefer than others, there is no hierarchy. The truth is that lots of people can manage the little things, and fewer people are able to take on the challenges of larger endeavors. That's okay! Think of this as a portrait of our collective

IN 30 SECONDS OR LESS

CONNECT

STAY IN TOUCH; MAKE IT LAST

STAND UP, ACT UP

START SOMETHING

efforts. Each new thing you try may lead to more new things, or you may inspire others to reach out to kids. The important thing is to explore the possibilities and find yourself somewhere in the picture. You may discover that you're already doing significant things without even realizing it. If you only have the time and energy to participate in brief moments of support and connection, do that. If you have the inspiration and resources to lead something larger, do that. Whatever you contribute will strengthen the web that surrounds the young people in your life.

I will provide you with true stories, successful strategies, and practical advice. The rest is up to you. Are you ready to change kids' lives?

In 30 Seconds
or Less

Make the most of brief interactions with youth.

It is threads, hundreds of tiny threads, which sew people together through the years.

SIMONE SIGNORET

So often we find ourselves saying, "I don't have time" or "I wish I had more time." Teachers work long hours at night, grading papers and preparing lesson plans. Parents race between home, school, and work, experiencing every responsibility at breakneck speed. Spending time with friends or extended family begins to feel like a luxury. Many people don't even know their neighbors' names. Who has time to change a kid's life?

This chapter serves as proof that even if you don't have more than a few fleeting moments, you can make all the difference in the world. One of the great secrets of life is the power of a word, a gesture, a look—at just the right moment. And nowhere is this truth more obvious—and more transformative—than when an adult makes the choice to connect with a child or teenager. It's the poetry of human development. Even the smallest efforts can have inspiring results.

Feeling valued is a crucial part of human development. Kids need to believe that they matter to adults—to the teachers, shop-keepers, neighbors, police officers, program leaders, and others who make up their communities. What kinds of things create this perception? Pose this question to young people, and they'll say it's simple stuff: eye contact, being asked for their opinions, being invited to contribute, having people call them by name, being noticed, receiving praise—even being reprimanded, when it's done with respect. And kids will also tell us how rarely these small gestures of life support actually occur.

A few years ago in Colorado I spoke at a town forum about Developmental Assets and the power of mobilizing citizens to take the time to notice, name, and support kids. An elderly woman stood up and said, "I live in a senior housing complex with 500 residents. We're all pretty healthy, but no kids live near us. I'm going to get everyone at my complex to promise that when they are out shopping, walking, or eating and they see a kid, to make eye contact and smile." Sounds small, doesn't it? It is small, but boy did it matter. She did mobilize 500 seniors. They did what they each promised. Two months later, teenagers reported that something odd was happening in their town. "People now look at me and smile. Are they laughing at me? Do I look funny?" One year later, teenagers stopped thinking of it as unusual; this kind of attention had become common practice. It just happens. It's in the DNA of the city. It's part of the culture. And it makes so many other good things easier to start, like conversations and authentic relationships. We're talking about small, sometimes tiny acts of hospitality. Door openers. Catalysts.

If you're still not convinced that a brief moment can make a difference, read the following three stories. They are all written in the first person; the first two are from the perspectives of adults looking back on their youth, and the third is told by an adult who was shocked by the impact of her small efforts.

A New Outlook

Tenessa Gemelke directs the publishing unit at Search Institute in Minneapolis. Her life took a leap forward when a school counselor gave her a new image of herself:

> *As the school year came to a close in the spring of 1990 at Marshall Junior High School in Marshall, Minnesota, all of the 400 students were required to attend the annual awards ceremony in the gymnasium. I was finishing my last year there. I had participated in a few extracurricular activities, but I was sure I wasn't on anyone's radar. I sat quietly while the obvious candidates accepted their awards.*
>
> *Then Mary Muchlinski, our school counselor, approached the podium to present the biggest award. Faculty members had nominated students and voted to recognize one outstanding boy and one outstanding girl in grade 8. As Mrs. Muchlinski began describing the female recipient, it gradually dawned on me that this person was starting to sound like me.*
>
> *Mrs. Muchlinski was extremely friendly and enthusiastic, but she was certainly not "cool," especially when*

she tried to get boys and girls mingling at school dances. She was the kind of person who seemed to know everybody's name, but I was still surprised one day early in the year when she stopped me in the hallway to ask if I would be running for student council. I explained that my friend was running, and I didn't want to oppose her. What I didn't say was that I secretly really wanted to be a student council member. I enjoyed working for the school newspaper and participating on the speech team, and I knew I would have loved student council. But I hardly had any friendships, and I wasn't about to jeopardize the few I had. I kept all of this to myself. Honestly, I'm sure our conversation lasted less than a minute. I hardly interacted with Mrs. Muchlinski at all throughout the rest of the year.

So there I sat at the awards ceremony, listening to her describe an award-winning student who sounded more and more like me. She confirmed my suspicions when she told the story about student council. I couldn't believe she even remembered that conversation, much less thought it was important! I'll never forget her final words before announcing my name: "This person stepped aside to support her friend's opportunity to be in student council. Sometimes the best leaders are the ones who encourage leadership in others."

I was stunned by this interpretation. I hadn't realized it, but this woman had truly paid attention to me. She understood my awkwardness, my love of learning, and my longing to fit in. I had found that year to be terribly lonely, but she stood up in front of the whole school and somehow managed to declare it a success story—an award-winning one!

One small gesture can introduce a new outlook into the life of a lonely young person.

When Mrs. Muchlinski announced my name and my fellow students congratulated me that day, my self-esteem went through the roof. My whole perspective changed. I entered high school the next year with unex-

*pected confidence and optimism. It's no
exaggeration when I tell you that Mrs.
Muchlinski's words changed the course
of my life. I learned from her that one
small gesture from a caring adult can
introduce a new outlook into the life of
a lonely young person.*[1]

The Voice of Respect

Mike Clark started and directs the Center
for Strength-Based Strategies in Mason,
Michigan. With one simple act, he
reclaimed his name, and with it, his dignity.

*My story comes from a life-changing
event on a basketball court when I was
13 and in junior high school in Howell,
Michigan. I was overweight and terribly self-conscious as a young boy. I
grew up in a large family, the seventh
son with six older brothers. One day
during an after-school basketball game,
I crashed into my older brother, who
was driving to the basket for a lay-up. I
wasn't as coordinated as I would have
liked, and my obvious bumping foul
angered my brother. He yelled, "If it*

wasn't for you, Porky, I would've made that shot!"

The game ended, and as we rode away on our bikes an older boy from our neighborhood called out, "Hey, what was that name your brother called you?" I shrugged and hoped that if I didn't answer, the question would die. To my dismay he answered his own question by yelling, "Porky!" Everyone laughed, and the nickname stuck.

This nickname became so commonplace that many students in my school did not know my given first name! I tried to make the best of it, saying it helped me meet people and that a nickname made me approachable by helping people feel more at ease. What a self-soothing justification. The real truth was, it hurt. The nickname became universal when I happened to take the stage at a school rally. As a homeroom representative, I was assigned to make a short address to all grades assembled. To my shock, my homeroom teacher introduced me as "Porky Clark." My humiliation was complete. As I approached *the podium, the laughter and catcalls were overwhelming, yet I smiled and waved to the assembly, trying to show that I was comfortable and confident. Inside I was crying.*

The following year when classes began, I was placed in an English class with a young teacher who was new to our school. With her high energy level and infectious enthusiasm, Mrs. Narda Murphy was destined to become well liked. At the start of the first day of class, she began by taking the class roll call. Moving through the alphabet, she reached my name and called out, "Mike Clark?" I was shocked to hear my real first name being used in front of my peers. I eventually raised my hand and answered, "Here." No one heard my response as a whole classroom burst into laughter. My teacher looked around, puzzled, and asked, "What's so funny?" A voice in the back yelled, "That's not Mike Clark, that's Porky!"

She slowed and simply said, "Oh, I see." Then she turned to me and said with a soft voice, "What would you like to be called?" I froze; no one had ever asked me that question before. I eventually found my voice through the snickers and answered, "Mike." "Then 'Mike' it will be," she replied with a strength that quieted the group, and she used my given first name from that point forward.

Her act alone did not bring an end to the nickname. It stuck around until my high school graduation. Yet that day in her classroom began a turnaround for me. I was drawn to this teacher, minded her rules, and worked hard for her. Beyond the class, I know she started my lifelong process of becoming "me." That morning I felt something awaken within me. How could I have known that this would begin a self-rally that would transcend not only the nickname but some of life's greater obstacles to follow? My teacher's affirmation, simply endowing me with my own name, sparked the more resil-

The most enduring gifts we give might well be shrouded in simple moments of respect.

*ient part of me, allowing me to better
insulate myself from hurtful comments
and to begin figuring out how to have
an impact in life.*

*I eventually developed a career
dedicated to youth, working for 20 years
as a juvenile probation officer. Mrs.
Murphy gave me the gifts of learning
to be present with youth and helping
to introduce them to their own "I can
overcome" successful side. Her act helped
me to understand that the most enduring gifts we give might well be shrouded
in simple moments of respect, acknowledgment, and affirmation.*[2]

A Chance Encounter

Flora Sánchez is a veteran educator and
trainer in Albuquerque, New Mexico. She
has told this story in hundreds of workshops
and speeches:

*It was a gorgeous day in late fall when
I decided to make a quick stop at the
grocery store on my way home from
work. About a week before I'd attended
a Safe and Drug Free Schools confer-*

32

*ence in Washington, D.C., where
I heard a keynote introducing the
idea of Developmental Assets. What
impressed me most was the idea that my
intentional efforts could really make a
difference in a young person's life. As I
gathered my groceries many days later, I
was still thinking about that speech.*

*As I stood at the checkout counter
while the cashier rang up my purchases,
I happened to glance to the side and
notice the young girl who was bagging my groceries. A key phrase about
Developmental Assets popped into
my head: "Take advantage of every
moment." I instantly made the decision
to reach out to this girl. Noting her
nametag, I said her name, "Maria."
She looked up at me and I tried to
make eye contact to give her a smile,
but she had long hair that fell over her
face, so I couldn't see her eyes. I felt a
little awkward, grasping for something
positive to say, so I paid her the first
genuine compliment that came to mind:
"Thank you for bagging my groceries so
carefully. It's nice to get home with my*

eggs intact and my bread not crushed."
She acknowledged me with a little nod
and continued bagging my groceries.
When she was done, I made another
attempt to connect, saying, "Maria,
thank you. You're a great sacker."

Then Maria asked if she could help
me take the groceries to the car. I think
of myself as an able-bodied woman, so
I ordinarily say "no" when asked if I
need help. But the store wasn't too busy,
and I was glad Maria seemed responsive,
so I accepted her offer. On the way to
my car I asked her a few questions. Do
you like working at Albertson's? What
high school do you attend? What grade
are you in? Are you looking forward
to anything coming up in school? She
responded in a quiet little voice, never
looking at me. I could barely hear her
over the thump, thump of the grocery
cart wheels on the parking lot pavement,
but by then I was fully determined to
listen well, so I leaned in and paid close
attention to her responses.

Soon we arrived at my car and
unloaded my groceries. As I closed the

trunk, I took one more opportunity to reach out: "Maria, it's been nice getting to know you a little. Thank you for your help this afternoon." And then, she suddenly looked up at me and pulled her hair back over her ear. I noticed that she had tears in her eyes as she said something that I will never forget, "No, thank you. Most people don't even know I'm here."

As I climbed into my car and drove away that fall day I had a huge "aha" moment. It had worked! That moment was transformational for me. Connecting with youth can be so simple and so easy—taking almost no extra effort or time. I was standing at the checkout stand anyway. I was walking to my car anyway. It took very little extra effort to reach out and relate to a young person, someone I didn't even know. I enjoyed it and felt good doing it. And most importantly, judging from her reaction, it seemed to matter to Maria. I realized then that reaching out to children and teenagers could be part of every aspect of my life—personal, profes-

sional, and informally with every young person I encountered.

But that's not where my story ends.

Years later I was invited to participate in a panel to discuss education issues in our community. As the date grew closer, I almost called and opted out—I was way too busy. I'm so very glad I didn't cancel, because that night something remarkable happened. The meeting was well attended; we had a great discussion and interaction from participants. But I was in a hurry to get home when it was over, so I rushed out and was almost to the front door of the building when a voice from down the hall called out, "Ms. Sánchez, can I talk to you for a minute?" I turned to see a beautiful young woman approaching, her high heels clicking on the linoleum hallway floor. When she was nearer she said, "You don't remember me, do you?" I looked closely at her. Her hair was pulled back in a ponytail, she had gorgeous brown eyes and a great smile—but no, I didn't recognize her. I struggled for a moment trying to think of a grace-

ful way to admit this when she blurted, "My name is Maria, and fourteen years ago I was a sacker at Albertson's grocery store." I was dumbfounded. Shocked. Incredulous. I shook my head in absolute disbelief to see her again.

She continued quickly, "I didn't know your name then, but when I saw you tonight and heard your voice, I knew it was you. And I knew that I wanted to tell you what was going on with me that day. You see, exactly one week before that day I was raped. It was a date rape, and I was feeling such guilt and shame that I'd just stuffed everything else deep down inside. I hadn't told a soul, not even my parents. I hadn't even cried. But after you drove off that day, all of a sudden, out of nowhere, the tears came. I cried and cried; I cried till I shook. I knew I needed to return to the store and get back to work, but I couldn't stop crying. And so I went around the parking lot collecting all the empty grocery carts, trying to collect my composure. As I did, an amazing thought came to me:

*if a stranger can seem to care about
me, surely my parents will understand
and support me. And so I made up my
mind to tell them that evening. And I
did. They told me they loved me and
would always support me. They went
with me to the Rape Crisis Center. And
fourteen years later I'm healing, and I
just wanted to say thank you."*

*Of course, by then I was in tears
myself; so was she. We held each other
for a few seconds and then I asked her
to join me at a restaurant nearby so we
could talk more. Over a cup of coffee I
shared what our encounter had meant
to me. I told her that as I drove away,
I was struck by how much our brief
interaction had seemed to affect her. I
told her that I'd
given hundreds
of presentations
over the years,
and in almost
every one I'd told
the "Maria the
grocery sacker"
story. I told her*

**Although many of
us perform simple
acts toward young
people—reaching
out, listening, sup-
porting, encour-
aging—we wonder
whether it makes
a difference.**

*that often audience members come up
to me afterward, telling me they'll never
overlook the opportunity to say hello
and thanks to any young person who
serves them. Maria smiled then, and I'll
carry that lovely smile with me for the
rest of my days.*

*This story was a rare gift to me. It
made me realize that although many
of us perform simple acts toward young
people—reaching out, listening, supporting, encouraging—we wonder
whether it makes a difference. The
chance event of Maria attending that
community meeting that night and
deciding to reconnect with me meant
that I was rewarded with the knowledge
that even a small gesture of noticing can
make a huge difference.*

These three stories remind us that life-
changing gifts often come in very small
packages, delivered by people who simply
make a mental note to connect, look for
opportune moments, and spring into action.
Imagine what could happen if we all took
this approach.

Finding Your Way, 30 Seconds at a Time

These stories illuminate three important principles. Each is central for raising great kids in our society. And each typically gets too easily discounted. They are as follows:

- *One small effort does matter.* Little things such as using names, making eye contact, saying hello, expressing gratitude, and simply starting a conversation are a big deal. You never know which encounter will change a young person's life.

- *Small acts add up.* Kids can't get enough of this kind of attention. These efforts connect young people to place, tradition, and the possibilities in life. This is how we show them they belong, they matter, and they are valuable. These moments are like threads that unite to create a beautiful tapestry.

- *If you breathe, you are on the team.* Regardless of your profession or your family status, you are a resource for kids. Slow down. Pay attention. Act.

Remember, the experience of feeling valued isn't about programs, school curricula, or city policy. It has to do with how we adults carry ourselves—what we notice and how we respond. No amount of money or legislation can make it happen. It is a matter of personal and collective will. Remember the examples in this chapter, and use even the briefest moments to take action.

The Parent Perspective

As you consider making these additional efforts, you may worry that parents would disapprove if you got involved with their children. This is a common fear among caring adults, so Search Institute put this idea to the test. With the help of Gallup, we conducted a national study of parents and other adults. The study was called *Grading Grown-Ups: How Do American Kids and Adults Relate?*[3] The results were surprising. Parents, it turns out, are *more likely* than other adults to believe it is important for unrelated adults to be involved in kids' lives in positive and mean-

> **Parents want safe, caring adults to surround their kids.**

WATCH OUT FOR **CREEPS**

When it comes to relationships between adults and young people, we often find ourselves paralyzed by suspicion or distrust. Why is your neighbor so friendly? Is it okay to let your son go somewhere alone with a mentor? Why does the coach pay so much individual attention to the players? In short, how do you know who is safe and who isn't?

Unfortunately, child predators do not wear warning labels. Although there is no guaranteed way to protect youth from danger, there are several things you can do to increase the safety in youth-adult relationships:

- **Get to know the adults in your child's life.** When you drop your child off somewhere, stop and chat for a few minutes. If you don't know one of your child's friends well, invite the other family over so the parents can get to know each other.

- **Insist on background checks.** Many youth programs already have mandatory background checks for all staff and volunteers. Contact a local law enforcement agency if you need more information.

- **Check references.** If your child is spending time with someone you don't know well, talk to someone who does know that person. "What is she like? How well do you know her?" Don't be afraid to ask questions until you feel confident that your child is safe.

- **Set boundaries.** Tell adults what you expect when they spend time with your child. Be explicit about the things that matter to you: "Please have her home at 7:30." "I don't allow him to watch violent movies." Seek out adults who respect these boundaries.

- **Coach your child.** Help children and teens learn how to determine which adults are safe. Teach them what to do when they feel uncomfortable in a situation.

- **Trust your instincts.** If you're getting a bad vibe from someone, listen to that voice in your head. You don't have to leave your child with someone you don't trust.

- **Encourage relationships with adults you already know well.** Help your child build a stronger friendship with someone familiar— one of your own friends, a favorite aunt, a youth group leader. Reach out to the people you appreciate and respect.

Whatever you do, don't give up on connecting young people with safe adult friends. Caution is healthy, but isolation is not. All children need love and support from adults they can trust.

For more information about promoting healthy family relationships, visit parentfurther.com. For more information about protecting young people from abuse, visit preventchildabuse.org or stopit now.org.

HOW TO AVOID
BEING CREEPY

Just as parents may feel anxious about their children having contact with people who are not safe, adults often feel wary about reaching out to other people's kids. A caring adult may fear being seen as a pest, a weirdo, or even a predator.

Rather than avoiding relationships with young people altogether, try the following ideas to make yourself and others more comfortable with intergenerational friendships:

- **Get to know the parents first.** Before you engage in conversation with a young neighbor or one of your child's friends, establish trust with that young person's parents. Show that you are caring, kind, and approachable.

- **Listen more than you talk.** Excessive conversation and prying questions may seem aggressive. Allow time for young people to develop a comfort level instead of interrogating them immediately.

- **Be clear about your intentions.** Do you want to encourage a child's love of music? Are you worried about a teen who is transferring to a new school? How would you like to help? Be upfront about your reasons for wanting to be a friend.

- **Avoid isolation.** Even if you have the best intentions, a young person may feel uncomfortable being alone with you. Spend time in public places or with groups of people. Encourage young people to call home and check in with their families. Set conditions that make both parents and children feel safe.

- **Respect boundaries.** Help young people adhere to their families' rules and curfews. Show parents that you are a partner in reinforcing the values and expectations that matter to them.

- **Join a formal mentoring program.** Programs offer training and clear guidelines about appropriate behavior. You may also need to go through a criminal background check, reassuring kids and parents of your history as a safe person.

Reaching out to offer your support to a young person is one of the most powerful actions you can take. Although you may need to leave your comfort zone initially, you'll soon find that you're making an important, positive difference in someone's life.

For more information about being a mentor, visit search-institute.org/mentoring.

ingful ways. Although parents can't help but be frightened when they hear tales of child predators, they still recognize the value of "the village." Parents want safe, caring adults to surround their kids.

If you are a parent, you can purposefully invite trusted friends to form relationships with your kids. If you are an adult who would like to befriend a child, reach out to parents and make sure they know you and feel comfortable with your involvement.

We do have to recognize a danger that lurks in many communities. There is a small percentage of adults—and I mean small— who pose a danger to kids. Some are violent or sexual predators. Others may not pose such extreme hazards but still may not be good role models or examples for young people. So vigilance is important. Building trusted relationships with other adults is important. Teaching our kids about safety is important. While we have to recognize this problem, we can't afford to let the bad apples win. When fear rules, we let the small percentage of hurtful adults pollute the whole process of child development.

In 30 Seconds or Less:
30 Ideas for Action

There are plenty of ways you can start taking action today. You may want to seek parental consent for a few of the more personal efforts, and not every opportunity will be right for you. The important thing is to step outside of your own comfort zone and find as many chances as possible to show kids they matter.

1. When you pass kids on a sidewalk, make eye contact and wear an expression that suggests you're glad they are on the planet.

2. Learn the names of your friends' kids and your kids' friends.

3. Ask a teen to recommend a book, movie, or video game.

4. Cheer for kids who perform in public. Donate money to young musical groups or street performers.

5. Kneel, squat, or sit so you are at eye level with young children.

6. Admire artwork; it's okay to "ooh" and "ahh" if the artist is very young, but remember to give sincere compliments when you like what you see.

7. When you see a kid working hard at something, say how impressed you are.

8. Praise parents when they set clear boundaries, communicate kindly with their children, or show other signs of good parenting.

9. When you see new kids in your neighborhood, introduce yourself.

10. When you see acts of aggression, point out another way of solving the conflict.

11. Remember birthdays. Send a card to an introvert, or sing "Happy Birthday" to an extrovert.

12. Invite neighborhood kids to run through your sprinkler or use your basketball hoop.

13. Use chalk to write a welcoming message on your sidewalk. Invite young neighbors to add to the message with pictures and words of their own.

14. If you are a parent, thank any adult who matters to your kids.

15. When you see an act of racism or hear a slur, speak up.

16. Congratulate kids on their firsts and lasts, like the beginning and end of a school year or a sports season.

17. Send messages of support and encouragement. Use social networking and other technology in addition to handwritten notes.

18. Give kids a warm welcome when they enter your place of business.

19. Let parents and kids in your neighborhood know that your home is a "safe house"—someplace they can go for help or extra support.

20. Buy Girl Scout cookies even if you already have some.

21. Buy a glass at every lemonade stand, even if you're not thirsty.

22. If you see a kid in danger, be the person who intervenes or calls 911.

23. Avoid forcing yourself to use slang; an insincere "wassup" is just irritating.

24. If a child you know collects certain items, find something you can contribute to the collection.

25. Don't judge a young person's tattoos and piercings—better yet, compliment them!

26. Treat older teenagers like adults when you meet them: shake hands, ask them about their plans, and ask them for help or for their opinions and advice.

27. Encourage young people's interests when giving gifts: good art supplies, nice pens, sheet music, recorded music.

28. If you're aware of a young person's accomplishments, mention it in your "status" message on Facebook or Twitter—or whatever social-networking forum replaces those in the next ten minutes!

29. Stop what you're doing when kids walk through the door, and offer your full attention.

30. Thank coaches, mentors, teachers, and other adults who make these 30-second differences.

Connect

Begin to build transformative relationships.

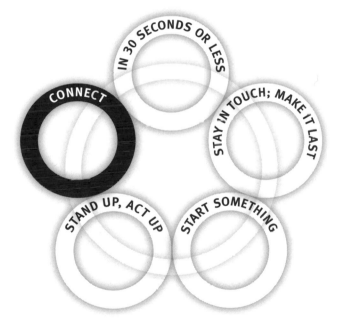

The meeting of two personalities is like the contact of two chemical substances: if there is any reaction, both are transformed. CARL JUNG

I have a grandson named Ryder. By all standards and measures known to humankind, he's awesome. Maybe even perfect. When he was 4, I overheard this conversation with his grandmother (a.k.a. Mō´-mah) out on our deck:

> Ryder: "Hey, Moma, ask me why I'm skipping."
>
> Moma: "Okay, Ryder, why are you skipping?"
>
> Ryder: "Because I'm so happy to be in the world."

Isn't that about as good as it gets? I'm not sure how and why my grandson is in this self-affirming frame of mind, but I'll bet it has something to do with all the people in his life who are cheering him on. He's got parents, neighbors, teachers, uncles, aunts, friends—and did I forget to say grandparents?—in his corner. It is a network of support, safety, formal and informal education, inclusion, tolerance for noise and acting out, praise, guidance, and, above all, exuberance for who he is.

I would love to bottle the confidence of age 4 so that he could drink from it when he's 8, 12, or 16. Things change. The path gets bumpy. People get busy. And before too long, many children become disconnected and lonely. I have heard it said that the most extreme form of punishment is isolation. On the flip side, the greatest gift we can give someone is connection.

> **"When adults are asked to look back on their lives and name the things that mattered most for their success and happiness, no one ever names a program. They always name relationships."**

As stated earlier, relationships are the oxygen of human development. Without them, we suffocate. But there is a poignancy and credibility when someone shows up in your life and chooses to connect with you.

My friend Bill Milliken founded Communities in Schools about 30 years ago. It has grown into a network of hundreds of schools that provide comprehensive health and mentoring support for kids who fall between the cracks. In every keynote speech I've heard Bill give, there is one common message: "When adults are asked to look back on their lives and name the things that mattered most for their success and happiness, no one ever names a program. They always name relationships." In his powerful book *The Last Dropout: Stop the Epidemic*, Milliken tells the story of Reggie Beaty. Growing up as a young person in Atlanta in the 1960s, Reggie struggled with the challenges of life in a community marked by poverty and violence:

> By the eighth grade, Reggie was into it all. You didn't hear the term "gangs" too much back then, but gang activity is what it was. Reggie carried a .22 and a .38 when he was 14 years old; robbery and drug addiction were an accepted part of his world.
> School was the next thing to go. In the ninth grade, he was expelled. "I started a life of crime," he'll tell you bluntly. For two years he was in and

out of juvenile detention, usually for breaking and entering, sometimes for drug dealing. People in the community who knew him kept saying: "Reggie, you're too smart for this. What happened to all that potential you had?" But as far as Reggie was concerned, the normal world—especially school—had given up on him, and he had no interest in trying to find a way back in.

Then one day while he was hanging with his friends and playing basketball when he should have been at school, two older guys started hanging around too. Like Reggie, they were African American, but he'd never seen them before. They definitely weren't from Bankhead Courts. These two guys kept showing up, and after a while they explained why: They said that they were "street workers" and they were starting something called a "Street Academy" for kids who had left school. It was a way to get back inside the system and get that diploma—but in a very different environment. The academy was small (never more than 100 students at any

one time), and the learning was inten-
sive and geared to the personal pace of
each young person.

At first Reggie took a pass on it,
but then a couple of young women he'd
grown up with—both of them now
teenage mothers—said they were going
to enroll in Academy T, as it was called.
The "T" stood for "Transition." After a
bit, they told Reggie: "You really should
consider this. It's making a difference.
These guys are okay." And the two street
workers, Bobby Garrett and Dave
Lewis, kept coming back to that basketball court. Basically, they wouldn't leave
Reggie alone. They kept bugging him
about giving Academy T a try.

Reggie has told me that he probably
would have gone over to the storefront
building that housed the academy and
checked it out, just out of curiosity, even
if he hadn't started to feel a connection
with the men who kept encouraging
him. He might even have enrolled on
his own. But he never would have made
it to graduation without Bobby Garrett,
who became his mentor. Academy

T was a great program. But, more important, Bobby gave Reggie a great relationship, and that was what made the difference.

Bobby's decision to connect with Reggie dramatically changed his trajectory. Once Reggie held himself accountable to the high expectations of a trusted mentor, he saw new possibilities and went on to achieve things he had never imagined:

From here on, Reggie's story sounds like something I'm making up, but every word is true. He became president of the United Negro College Fund at Stillman, vice president of his fraternity, and president of his dormitory. He served on the mayor's advisory council and commanded the ROTC drill team. He received a full scholarship for the next three years as a result of his outstanding abilities in ROTC. By the end of his career at Stillman, Reggie was commander of the entire ROTC program. And he entered the Army as a commissioned officer, a second lieutenant.

Reggie's love of teaching flourished while he was in the military, with superb results: He was named the nation's best ROTC instructor in any college or university, and his work with youth in Oklahoma earned him "Man of the Year" honors. He chaired fund-raising committees for charity groups, started a mentoring program for young minority officers, and commanded a battalion of 2,000 soldiers.

Think of the difference people like Bobby Garrett make. Part mentor, part friend, part advocate, Bobby transformed a life and gave our nation a leader. His commitment of time and energy paid off in ways he never anticipated. Looking back on the experience, Reggie reflected, "My relationship with a caring adult saved my life."[1]

Who, Me? Yes, You!

If I had a magic wand and could make one thing happen in our world, it would be to ensure that every kid had a network—a web of trusted, safe, caring adult relationships. The adults in this network would simply show up, hang around, peer into kids' souls, and let those young people know that they want to be around them. It is in this crucible of relationships that youth confront challenges, tell stories, develop values, transfer wisdom, make meaning, overcome obstacles, and discover the sparks within them.

As a social scientist who thinks about this stuff a lot—and has done so for a long time—I wish every adult would ponder four things:

1. There are millions of kids who have no one on their team.

2. There are millions of kids who have one or two parents on their team, but no one else.

3. There are millions of kids who have some relationships but not enough.

4. Relationships with kids are additive: the more, the better.

Meaningful connections with kids can happen anywhere and can be initiated by anyone. Some years ago, Search Institute published a study in which teenagers were asked whom they would turn to first if they needed advice or support. The answer was something of a surprise. The clear number one choice was "the parent of one of my friends."[2] Remember that experience? When we were young, we knew other kids' parents who seemed more approachable—and perhaps less judgmental—than our own. If you are a parent, keep your eyes open for opportunities to connect with the friends of your kids—and don't be surprised if your kids are more open with other parents than they are with you. The important thing is to surround all kids with the support they need.

> **Don't be surprised if your kids are more open with other parents than they are with you.**

Ways to Reach Out

Each connection requires a first step and a touch of courage to initiate that deeper connection. The next section offers several examples of ways adults have chosen to reach out to young people. These gestures go beyond the simple interactions described in the first chapter. Whether formal or informal in nature, these stories illustrate the difference between simply express-ing kindness and discovering genuine connection.

- Sharon Sayles Belton, a big-city mayor for eight years and now a founda-tion executive, bakes cookies every Saturday morning for neighborhood kids. They keep coming back for the cookies and the conversation.

- In St. Louis Park, Minnesota, the adults in the community—some who have kids and some who simply want to be good neighbors—wait with kids at school bus stops in the morn-ing. They use this opportunity to just be present, hang out, have a cup of coffee, and start conversations. The idea has spread. My daughter and her husband (parents of Ryder) recently moved to a nearby community. When the new school year started, they began seeing a gathering of neighbors every morning down at the corner, as many as 20 on any given morning.

When asked why they do this, the easy response was, "It's just the way people on our street let kids know they matter to all of us."

- Nicole Mattson was a college student spending her summer at home in a small town in North Dakota. She couldn't apply for a job during her temporary stay, so she put an ad in the local newspaper, offering her services as a tutor. One father responded to her ad, asking if she could work with his son, Tyler. Tyler was a 5-year-old who had been legally blind since birth, but he had just undergone an operation to restore his vision. Nicole spent the summer working with him on shapes and colors, numbers and letters. Nicole had no professional training, and she points out that this was several years ago, "back when the Internet had barely been invented." The two of them simply worked hard and had fun preparing for kindergarten in the fall. Tyler is now a senior in high school, and he has been on the honor roll every year. His father still credits Nicole with being the person who set him on a course for success.

- Once a year, Chris Fisher and Patty Hoolihan and their children gather with a group of music-loving adults and youth for an evening of making music. Invitees bring a food dish— and an instrument—to share, and the evening takes off. The only rule is that each person has to perform at least one piece, but the piece can be done with someone else or several others. It can even be as simple as playing the old piano standby, "Chopsticks." This common love of music has given Patty the opening to connect with one young musician whom she might not know if he didn't come to the event. Now when she sees him at school or in the neighborhood, she always asks him how he's doing with the trombone.

Think about the many opportunities you have in your own life to initiate these types of connections. What talents or interests might you share? Where can you show up and reach out?

The Power of Volunteer Coaches

Peter Scales is the Senior Fellow at Search Institute, a capacity in which he generates some of the most important research studies in the United States on positive youth development. But there's another side to him that gives me a lot of joy and makes him near and dear to my heart: Peter is a volunteer tennis coach at Parkway South High School in Manchester, Missouri. He spends hours every afternoon in the fall and spring honing the serves and ground-strokes of the next Roger Federers. (At least that's what some of his young players dream about.) But the pursuit of stardom is not why Peter coaches. He is much more interested in providing athletes with the support they need for healthy development. In his article "Building Your Tennis Players' Developmental Assets and Success for Life,"[3] Peter offers many recommendations for this positive approach to coaching:

- Take an interest not only in athletic skill development but also in participants' development as persons. Take every opportunity to talk about their interests, schoolwork, and plans for the future.

- Build connections to players' parents. Welcome them to matches, learn their names, and engage in dialogue with them, not only about their child's athletic development but about their other strengths and interests.

- Emphasize the value of helping others, not only on one's team, but also in the broader community.

- Reinforce positive expectations and boundaries for responsible behavior.

- Model the behavior you want to see in your athletes.

Some people become coaches out of a passion for the sport itself. Others find themselves roped into the role as their young kids get involved, learning the rules of the game along with the participants.

Whether you are a seasoned sports lover or a new recruit, take advantage of this role as the perfect opportunity to become a caring adult in the life of every player.

Relationships and the Process of Thriving

I love the concept of thriving. I know what a thriving plant looks like: it reaches up and out; it radiates beauty. It's discovering its full potential. Surprisingly, there has been very little research on *human* thriving—living a life that exudes joy and energy in becoming one's best self, a process that should begin in childhood and adolescence. Over the last decade, my colleagues and I at Search Institute have led a national initiative to define, study, and apply the concept of thriving to the way we raise kids in our communities.

> **Human thriving is living a life that exudes joy and energy in becoming one's best self, a process that should begin in childhood and adolescence.**

There are two central dynamics in a life of thriving. The first is the identification of one's *spark*. We use the word spark to describe the part of us that generates passion and purpose in life. It is the internal engine (or maybe even the internal flame) that animates our lives. *Spark* is akin to the word *spirit*, which, in its original Latin meaning, refers to "my breath." A spark comes from the inside of a person and is either allowed to flourish or is extinguished. A spark is much more profound than an interest or a hobby. It is a deep source of meaning and purpose. It's like a gift that has been entrusted to you.

One of the ways we conduct research on sparks is to ask this interview question:

> *"What is it about you that gives you joy and energy and is an important part of who you are? This is the human spark, the internal engine that lights your fire. A spark gives a person a sense that her or his life has purpose and direction. It might be writing, or science, or learning about nature, making music, being an artist, being a leader, helping others, running like the wind, or learning languages. Sparks are not just about things you like to do, like being with friends*

THE ART OF
CONVERSATION

All of us—as parents, teachers, mentors, and friends—know that some young people can present a conversational challenge. The question "How's it goin'?" gets nothing but a head nod or a grunt. The same with "Hey, how's school?" These questions just don't start the dialogue we're hoping for.

Robert Reich, who served as secretary of labor in the Clinton administration and who is now a professor of public policy at the University of California, Berkeley, has an interesting way of understanding the art of conversation with his teenage sons. He says that teenagers, particularly boys, are like clamshells. They are all closed up, but once in a while they open up. His advice: when the shell opens, be there and be ready, not with admonition or complaint, but a conversation starter that draws the young person in.

Here are some possibilities:

- Who's your best teacher at school? What do you like about that teacher?

- What is something you are afraid to try? How might you overcome that fear?

- What's one question you have about your family history?

- If you were in charge of planning meals for a week, what would be on the menu?

- How have you changed as a person in the last year?

- Have you ever gone through a difficult time with a friend? How did you resolve the situation?

- How could your school or community make you feel more included in decision making? Which decisions would you like to affect?

If you strike out with one question, try another one. Keep fishing for the one that will generate a moment of connection. *For more ideas, visit the Conversation Generator at search-institute.org/conversation-generator.*

or playing video games. A spark comes from a deeper place. It's yours to give the world. What is your spark?"

Our studies of thriving have involved nationally representative samples of more than 5,000 12– to 18-year-olds. This decade long initiative has included research partnerships with Tufts University, Stanford University, and the Ph.D. program in psychology at Fuller Theological Seminary in Pasadena, California. Across all of our work, we have found that kids understand the idea of sparks in a heartbeat.[4] They know what it feels like and looks like. They can spot which peers experience sparks and which ones don't. About two-thirds can quickly name their spark (and in some cases, several sparks).

In describing their sparks, young people frequently use the language of romance, as in *relish, love, passion, commitment,* and *sacrifice.* These are right-brain words of emotion rather than left-brain words of reason. Here are some examples of how teens describe their spark:

- "My spark is art. I love to paint and sculpt and make art out of pieces of junk."

- "I love reading about archaeology. I can go to a library, pull out a book, and lose all sense of time."

- "I feel so wonderful when I spend time with little children. It brings so much joy to my life."

Now let's get to the second part of the thriving formula: a young person's spark needs to be nurtured, just as a seed needs to land in rich soil in order to grow. The primary soil for sparks is relationship—and a particular kind of relationship. Our studies show that a young person's spark best flourishes when three adults know, affirm, and nourish it. New evidence suggests that there is added power when these "spark champions" are included among the young person's family, school, and community.

What happens when a young person has both a spark and adults who celebrate it? It should come as no surprise that the outcomes are compelling: increases in school success, compassion for others, and leadership, and decreases in violence and antisocial behavior.

Now here's the downer: for most kids in America, the spark is unseen, unacknowledged, and undernourished. When I ask young people about their sparks, I am personally struck by how often they reply, "You really want to know? No one's ever asked me this before."

> **A young person's spark best flourishes when three adults know, affirm, and nourish it.**

In one of our national studies, we discovered that only 35 percent of 12– to 18-year-olds report that there are adults at school who know their sparks. These percentages fall even lower for faith communities (23%), after school programs (21%), and neighborhoods (6%).

Our nation's kids are hungry for adults to see their light, their gift, their spark. And we so easily miss it—maybe because our own sparks have been extinguished.

To create a truly transformative relationship with your child, your student, your mentee, or your neighbor, I've created a list of seven potentially life-changing questions:

- What is your spark?

- When and where do you express your spark?

- Who knows about your spark?

- Who helps feed your spark?

- What gets in your way?

- How can I help?

- How will you use your spark to make our world better?

If you launch this dialogue—in one conversation or across several—don't be surprised if a young person turns the question around and asks you to define your spark. He or she may even push you to consider tough questions, such as, "What was your spark when you were my age? Did it change? Did you ever lose it?"

If you are willing to risk honesty and self-revelation in this connection with a young person, you have each entered cherished and uncommon territory. This dialogue is an opportunity to build an authentic relationship, a connection based on trust and truth, a conversation that nourishes a young person's soul—and yours. It's the kind of relationship kids hunger for and rarely have. Try it. It will build a bond that changes both of you.

Connect: 30 Ideas for Action

Which connections are you already making with youth? Are you connecting with your own children? Do you work in a classroom full of children or teenagers who need this kind of support? What about your neighbors? You realize connections are important, but it can be challenging to come up with tangible ideas. Look through the following list and identify opportunities you can take to have a deeper impact (you may need to seek parental consent for some of these ideas):

1. Text a message of encouragement or a simple "Good morning! I hope you have a wonderful day!" and do it

often. If you don't know how to send texts, ask a teen to teach you how.

2. Offer to tutor youth through community groups and library programs.

3. When kids are in trouble, help them find the phone numbers or locations of counselors or other service providers.

4. Organize informal activities (such as pickup basketball, horseshoes, build-your-own-sundae parties, Monopoly contests) with kids in your neighborhood.

5. Find out what a kid loves, whether it's sunsets, fireworks, or Dairy Queen treats. Enjoy life's pleasures with someone else who appreciates them.

6. Plan and prepare a meal with one of your children. Invite your child's friend to join you.

7. Ask a young person this question: "What book are you reading now?

May I borrow it after you're done?" Once you've read it, reconnect to discuss it. You may even consider starting a book club that includes teenagers as well as adults.

8. Find out if there is another adult who has connected well with your own child. Have they bonded over sports? Do they like the same music? If you can afford it, buy them tickets to attend an event together.

9. Give parents a break by offering to take young children to a park. Act like a kid while you're there.

10. Ask a teen this question: "What's your favorite music right now?" Listen to the recommended musician or song and talk about it.

11. Invite a young person to attend a ball game or a movie with you. Afterward, discuss the experience over ice cream.

12. Start this conversation: "How many nicknames have you been given? Which is your favorite? Are there any you dislike?"

13. Invite a young person to join you for a walk, a hike, or a bike ride. Quiet times like these are perfect opportunities to chat.

14. Start this conversation: "Who makes you laugh? Have you ever laughed so hard you thought you couldn't stop?"

15. Keep your home stocked with as many books and art supplies as possible to make it an inviting place for kids to learn.

16. Contact a school to find out if they need chaperones or volunteers for special events.

17. Whenever you get a chance, ask a teenager for an opinion on something you are struggling with (for example, a conflict in your office,

a school policy issue, a moral dilemma).

18. Start this conversation: "What's the best advice an adult ever gave you? What's the worst?"

19. Ask a young person to give you a hand with a home project.

20. Use Facebook, Twitter, and other social-networking platforms to communicate in genuine ways. A word of encouragement is worth a lot in any medium.

21. Start a conversation about a young person's spark. Ask what you can do to help nurture it.

22. If you know what a young person's spark is, pay attention! If it's visual art, go to a museum together. If it's community service, do a volunteer project together. Support this young person's sense of passion and purpose.

23. Create awards to recognize your kids and others for things they do well.

24. If you can afford it, pay for a kid to have an experience. For example, send a young person to a camp, a class, or a special school trip.

25. Offer to coach a teen in leading an event or a service project through a congregation or a program. Let the young person be in charge, but make yourself available for advice and problem solving.

26. If you are a board member or a leader within an organization, get youth involved in the annual program planning and other initiatives.

27. Listen first and refrain from giving advice. Instead, ask whether or not a young person would like your help.

28. Take time to discuss current events that impact young lives. Value every

perspective, whether it comes from a teenager or a 4-year-old.

29. Make a family "business card" for your household. Include contact information and a message about how you'd like to connect (gardening, going for walks, etc.). Give one to every neighbor family that has children or teens.

30. Be ready for unexpected moments of connection. When a young person starts to talk about something personal, drop everything to pay attention.

Stay in Touch;
Make It Last

*Let a young person know that your support
is unconditional and unending.*

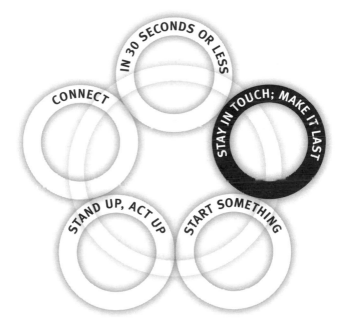

Love is knowing a person's song so well that you can hum it back to her on the days she can't remember the melody. MAYA ANGELOU

I t is one thing to build a relationship with a young person, but it gets exponentially better when we choose to connect over and over again with the same person. This kind of sustained relationship is an even greater source of strength and support. Later in this chapter I'll provide a wide range of examples, but first I want to talk about the important role teachers, coaches, and other professionals have in creating lasting connections.

Many people who interact with kids do so in programs or in schools. Sometimes this creates the perception that students or participants are just visiting—cycling through our systems and moving on to the next grade, the next team, or the next stage of life. The idea of "staying in touch and making it last" may sound daunting. I hope you'll learn from this next story that even small efforts can have a big payoff:

A few years ago, I struck up a conversation with Sarah, a 13-year-old who was in grade 8. It happened in a shopping mall, of all places, on a bench under a couple of indoor shade trees. She and I both found ourselves there one winter day. (If you know Minnesota, green, leafy trees in January are hard to come by.) After talking for a bit, I posed this question: "What's the best experience you've ever had in your life?" Sarah closed her eyes, went silent for a minute, and then replied in a voice tinged with emotion, "It happened right here, in this mall, about two months ago. It was when my fourth-grade teacher—who I hadn't seen in four years—walked up to me and called me by name."

Whoa! I thought she'd say the family vacation in California, or a canoe trip at a state park, or winning a gymnastics competition. Instead she chose a moment, a deeply human moment of reconnection. In Sarah's young and changing life, it was the experience of being known across time. She was cherishing what it was like to be remembered, to be visible, to be significant enough or worthy enough that an adult could— after what must have seemed like eons to a kid—draw a name out of her mental databank and say it. It must have been such a small gesture from her teacher's perspective, but it was a true gift to a young person in the process of figuring out if and how she matters in the world.

Whenever I talk about the power of sustained relationships, I start with the Sarah story. I did so recently in a keynote speech at a teacher conference in Orlando, Florida. What happened was unexpected and deeply emotional. I heard some noise in one corner of the room. A young teacher was sobbing. I stepped off the stage and approached her

> **She was cherishing what it was like to be remembered, to be visible.**

seat. I had a handheld microphone with me, and to my surprise, she took it. She had something important to say. Gathering herself, she said, "I can't believe this, but exactly the same thing happened to me. I was in the eighth grade. In a park that summer, Mrs. Guiterex, my fourth-grade teacher, found me and called me by name. It startled me that she remembered me and my name. It took my breath away. I decided right then to become a teacher like Mrs. G."

This is every speaker's fantasy—an audience member sharing an authentic story that reinforces your point. I was all set to go back to the podium when she touched my arm and said, "There's more. Mrs. G is here in this audience. I've never thanked her for remembering me and changing my life." With that, the young teacher runs over to hug her mentor, both of them crying, which of course makes the rest of the audience and me cry, too. It was an unbelievable testament to the lasting impact one person can have.

In a time when test scores and evaluation are what drives funding for schools and programs, it's important to remind ourselves that the capacity to really know a young person is a rare and valuable gift. When we ask adults to think back on the childhood experiences that most shaped them, they almost always mention individuals rather than activities, programs, or school subjects. And teachers are not the only individuals we recall. In fact, custodians, food service staff, and bus drivers are often the people who were constants in students' lives as they moved from grade to grade.

Never underestimate the power of human connection across time. These connections form the "web" of life. Each of us has the capacity to be part of the web for children and teens. The operative idea in this chapter is sustaining the connection. That means checking in now and then, showing up now and then, being in conversation now and then. And keeping it up for years.

> **Never underestimate the power of human connection across time.**

The Web of Connection

There is a lot of wisdom in our world about the power of a web. The word itself implies interconnection, strength, and a whole made of many parts.

Mary Francis works in Cincinnati, Ohio, in substance-abuse prevention—a field that depends on adults to surround young people with kindness and attention. In addition to being a resource to many youth, she shares a personal story about a few caring individuals who contributed their strands to her neighborhood's web:

*For eight years we have lived in the
same neighborhood beside a church
with an aging community. We attend
a different church, but we often greet
"visitors" who walk by our fence. When
my daughter, Bitia, was younger, she
and another neighbor girl would go to
the church parking lot with sidewalk
chalk and draw. The elderly women
who meet regularly at the church would
really make a fuss, complimenting the
artwork when they arrived. They got
to know the girls and call them by
name, listening with great enthusiasm
to stories about what the girls drew. The
women always thanked the girls for
sharing their talents.*

*Now that the girls are older and
have moved on to other activities, the
congregation members still stop by and
ask to see their current artwork. The
women wait by the fence as the girls run
in to get paintings and other creations
to share. Bitia very much looks forward
to seeing them and has commented that
this is what heaven must be like: people
noticing each other.*

Whether or not we participate in communities of religion or faith, it is compelling to hear a young person respond so warmly to this kind of interaction with adults. It's also a helpful reminder that kids don't outgrow the benefits of adults who pay attention.

> **Kids don't outgrow the benefits of adults who pay attention.**

In the United States, many stories about webs of relationships come from communities of color. I've heard former Secretary of State Colin Powell speak many times, often in his role as the founder of an organization called America's Promise. General Powell often speaks of the "Auntie-net" in his neighborhood in the Bronx when he was growing up. You couldn't go anywhere or do anything, he says, that was not observed by a host of women who constantly stuck their heads out their windows. If you did anything—bad or good—the Auntie-net would report it to your parents before you got home. This kind of sustained, intergenerational network of extended family has long been recognized as an important resource in African American families. Sociologist

Patricia Hill Collins describes this protective influence with the term "other mothers."[1]

When we look for examples among American Indian cultures, the web of support often spans multiple generations. Larry Brendtro and Martin Brokenleg describe it this way:

> In traditional tribal kinship systems, the siblings of one's parents would also be mothers and fathers, and the persons Europeans call cousins would be brothers and sisters. Most everyone with white hair would be a grandparent. Similar kinship models exist among tribal peoples worldwide, as reflected in the African adage "it takes a village to raise a child" and the Cree belief every child needs many mothers.[2]

I spent some time with Martin Brokenleg as we prepared to present at a conference with His Holiness the Dalai Lama. We were discussing the concept of compassion, and I offhandedly mentioned the Maya Angelou quote that is at the front of this chapter, "Love is knowing a person's song so well that you can hum it back to her on the days she can't remember the melody." Martin replied, "Among my people, we actually create a song for every child at birth. Our whole community knows each child's song, and at many points in a child's development, we sing it to him." What a beautiful example of sustained, collective relationships.

In addition to cultural values, we can look to scientific research for further evidence that young people benefit from a lasting circle of adult support. We know, for example, that a web of caring adults advances school success. The National Research Council states, "Supportive personal relationships are crucial to promoting and maintaining student engagement. Although learning involves cognitive processes that take place within each individual, motivation to learn also depends on the student's involvement in a web of social relationships that promote learning."[3] Across cultures, in neighborhoods and in schools, in informal networks and in professional programs, we see how weaving a web creates sustained connections over time.

The next section provides several examples of people just like you who are thinking of innovative ways to create these lasting connections with kids. Their efforts are natural and inspirational and unheralded. As you read these stories, think of ways you might take similar action in your own life.

Pen Pals

When her best friend's son, Willie, left for college, Karen Bartig spotted an opportunity to be a positive influence in his life.

> **Consistent correspondence is a surprisingly powerful force.**

Karen was well aware of how valuable a supportive adult could be to a young person, and she wanted to make sure that no matter how great the distance between them, Willie would still know how much she cared. She began writing letters.

Willie was a good writer who loved to correspond with family and friends. Karen kept in touch with him throughout the school year, and he always wrote back. She wrote about her daily life, sent postcards, and shared booklets and brochures from the various events she attended and places she visited.

Writing a simple letter may seem like a no-brainer, but consistent correspondence is a surprisingly powerful force. Karen noticed that she and Willie kept up with each other in writing in a way they never did when he lived nearby.[4]

The Power of Pancakes

Making pancakes for 25 middle school children every Friday morning before school was not something Nancy Slack ever deliberately thought about doing. She didn't set out to cook hundreds of pancakes as her son John and his friends made their way through grades 6 to 8 in their suburban neighborhood. When she was done, however, she had given—and received—a lot more than she ever imagined.

It all started because John wasn't quite ready for school one morning. The Slack family was new to their Portland, Oregon, community, and the middle school was only three blocks from their house. John's new buddies would swing by his house to pick him up every morning for the short walk to school. Sometimes John's friends would show up early before John was dressed, or John just wasn't quite together to walk out the door. Nancy asked one morning if the kids had had breakfast, and that's when she fired up the griddle. One Friday morning, she invited John's friends to plan on having breakfast, and the next thing she knew, she was cooking pancakes every Friday morning. As more young people got wind of things, a few more started showing up.

"I'd flip pancakes and pour juice," says Nancy. "They'd just forget I was there, listening in. I'd just stand there with a smile on my face. It was such an easy way to get to know these kids."

Nancy made pancakes through grade 7 when girls started to join the group and the dynamics changed. She flipped pancakes the day after one of the school's administrators—the designated disciplinarian, in fact—was publicly arrested for selling pot. She listened through the conversations when the students' favorite guidance counselor was hurt in a serious car accident.

"The pancakes were only the focus for a few of the kids who had started their growth spurts and wanted to eat. For most of them, it was about getting together and talking. As a result, I learned a lot about my son and had incredible relationships with these kids. I haven't made pancakes in three years, but there are young people at the high school who still greet me as 'Mom' as I walk down the hall."

By the time John and his friends started grade 8, Friday morning breakfast included a minimum of a dozen young people, and Nancy found herself making pancakes for as many as 25. She always kept things informal, letting kids know they were always welcome and making sure she had enough food for whoever might come. The front hall was a mountain of backpacks, and the kitchen was a train wreck afterward, but through it all, Nancy learned that just by being present, a caring adult can be a positive influence on her own children and their friends.

"It's really important to show kids they can have adults in their lives that they can talk to. I think it's important to just be available to them, to sit back and let them have a good time and not butt in. I just listened to their opinions and only offered mine if they asked for it. I was there, and I'm still there for them."[5]

Sowing Seeds

Julie Garrison lives on the East Coast. Her grandkids live 1,500 miles away. She sends care packages and talks to them on the phone, but she struggles for a consistent connection. This year she did something that may become a family tradition: she asked if she could plant flowers with her two young grandsons.

Instead of making this a one-time event, she tried to build up their excitement. She sent the packet of seeds as an Easter present and announced she'd be visiting in May. Then she flew out for Mother's Day weekend to help the boys do the planting. Now, whenever she talks to them on the phone, she always asks which ones are blooming and how big they've gotten. This is about continuity and closeness, in spite of geographical distance.

Knitted Together

Mary Ellen Buscher lives far away from her nieces and nephews, but she is an "honorary auntie" to her friend's son, Linus, who lives nearby. She knitted a beautiful cap when he was first born—soft and white with little lamb's ears. He quickly outgrew it, of course, but Mary Ellen was ready with a bigger hat just when he needed one. She has continued to make him new hats as he has grown. He is now 5 years old, and he still has a hat from his friend "Melly." Linus especially loves his current hat and frequently wears it outdoors—even in the heat of summer! People always notice how beautiful it is, and he proudly announces, "My friend made it for me. Melly makes the coolest hats!" Her thoughtful gifts have forged a lasting connection between the two of them.

The Gift of Literature

My wife, Tunie, is a lover of children's literature. She is a writer and reviewer and has an ever-growing collection of books for children and teens. And she loves to give books away. She has this uncanny knack of knowing which authors and illustrators kids in our neighborhood will find fun and compelling. She regularly delivers books to kids, and with several, she has a 10-year tradition going. Can you imagine how this then creates opportunities for conversation and connection? It's magic.

A Circle of Strength

When Eric Yancy and his wife decided to raise his 12-year-old brother, Eric quickly realized they couldn't do it alone. The boy was skipping school, running away from home, and stealing bikes. So the next time Eric met with four professional colleagues for their monthly career-support meeting, he told them about his brother. "They made a commitment right there that they would be involved in every turn of his life," Eric said. When Eric was traveling on business, these men would step in and attend school conferences, spend time with the boy, and give Eric's wife the support she needed. "They became the strong uncles," Eric said, "and they were right there."

These men became vital supports to the Yancy family, assisting them in negotiating through adolescence and helping Eric's brother graduate from high school and go on to Atlanta's Clark University. That set a pattern that has supported the family ever since. Now Yancy considers 18 people part of his extended family, though only two of them are biological. "We call them uncles and aunts," he says. "We have a little ceremony and then their names change" to Aunt and Uncle.[6]

Above and Beyond

Nancy Turner is a retired kindergarten teacher from Texas. She should go in the Relationship Hall of Fame. She taught for 35 years and had, I figure, 20 students each year. That multiplies out to 700 children. And she stays in touch with every one of them. She updates her address book, sends notes, and keeps her eye out for significant life events to celebrate. If a former student is in a play or a concert or a varsity game, she sends a note. She went to every high school graduation and quietly slipped a card and a $10 check into the hands of each of the graduates she taught 12 years earlier. It's not uncommon, she says, for a big, strapping high school graduate to break down and cry.

There's nothing better than the profound energy of a sustained relationship.

A Mentor's Long-Term Commitment

Moni was only 15 years old when she gave birth to her son. Fortunately someone at her school helped her connect with the Bright Beginnings mentoring program, a group geared especially toward supporting teen mothers. She met her mentor in the hospital on the day her son was born, and the two have been good friends ever since.

Moni is now 18 years old, and her son is a vibrant 3-year-old. The two of them have lived in five different homes in the past three years. They have struggled together through difficult family relationships and poverty, and the two of them are now living in a homeless shelter. Despite a tremendous number of obstacles, Moni has enrolled herself in nursing school and remains focused on a bright future for herself and her son.

Moni told her mentor, "It's people like you who keep me going. I can't always count on my mom or my baby's dad, but I just have to listen to the people who believe in me. Whenever I find anybody—a social worker, a doctor—who offers that extra support, I just keep calling that number when I need help. Your number is one of the only numbers I have memorized, so even if I lose my cell phone, I know I can still call you."

Calm in Crisis

Ellie Fralick of Rochester, New York, shares a story about a familiar face who was there when she needed him:

> *When I was 7, my 5-year-old sister Beezie died of leukemia just before Easter. We were the youngest of 5 children, and our older siblings were 12, 19, and 21. She had not been to school since Christmas, which I envied now and then, and was never hospitalized because my physician father felt more comfortable with her at home. Many of her transfusions and other care took place while I was at school, so I did not figure out how sick she was. And no one told me, really. The Tuesday before Easter my brother came home from college, which did not seem strange to*

me. No one told me that he was home because Beezie was going to die.

On Thursday, Beezie died while we were at school, and my aunt picked us up early and told us the news. When we got home later in the day, lots of things were going on, people coming and going, and I found it simpler to just stay upstairs. I was deeply puzzled by the goings-on. The wake was to be at home on Friday, which added to the activity in the house.

Saturday morning, the pace picked up again all around us. My next older sister and I were dressed and ready to go more than an hour before it was time to leave the house. My confusion mounted as I watched all the comings and goings from the dining room. The cars for the funeral procession were waiting, and the hearse was out front. My mother did what mothers so often do when a lot is going on; she said to go on outside and wait. Now I know that she had too much on her mind to deal with the two of us. I was happy to go out; it was too *crazy inside, and no one seemed to care about us.*

There was a policeman on a motorcycle outside, ready to lead at the head of the "parade." His name was Officer Moynihan, and he was the beat cop on the main street. He knew our family well because my brother went to school with his son. Alone, I walked over to Officer Moynihan to say hello. He called me by name. He was the friendliest man. I asked him, "Why are you here?"

His answer was spectacular: "I've come to lead the way to the church and make sure all the cars get there. Then I'm going to lead them all the way to the cemetery to make sure no one gets lost. And I'm going to wait there for you all. Then I'll make sure you all get home safely." He paused, then added, "I'm going to make sure you are safe."

I knew from that moment that I would always be safe. I would be safe in the weeks, months, and years ahead, no matter what my family faced. I never doubted it, because Officer Moynihan promised.

SUSTAINING THE **SPARK**

In the chapter titled "Connect," I mentioned the concept of the "spark," that hidden flame inside each young person that, by its very nature, is good, beautiful, and useful to the world. Connecting with a kid's spark is a great way to form a lasting relationship.

Once you've identified a young person's spark, try to be the person who offers long-term support:

1. Attend games, concerts, readings, or other public events to show your support for this important passion or talent.

2. Seek frequent updates about the young person's spark. Offer opportunities and suggestions, asking, "Have you written any new poems lately?" or "I heard there's a leadership camp scheduled next summer, and it made me think of you. Have you considered applying for it?"

3. If you possess a similar spark of your own, share this part of your life with a young person. Enter a 5K run together. Coauthor a letter to the editor of your local paper. Volunteer at an animal shelter.

Supporting a young person's spark is an easy but meaningful way to reconnect again and again. See appendix B or visit ignitesparks.com for more information.

Stay in Touch; Make It Last:
30 Ideas for Action

Which of the stories in this chapter have inspired you? Which actions seem daunting? Take some time to reflect on the opportunities in your own life. As you read the following list, consider what you might do to offer sustained love and support to a child or teenager you know:

1. Find out what a kid's favorite food is. Make a point of preparing it once a year as a birthday gift.

2. Give a kid a nickname. If she or he likes it, use it over and over again.

3. Send frequent postcards, even if you live in the same town or city.

4. Stay in touch with kids who spend time in your classroom or program. Even a simple greeting every now and then might make a huge impact.

5. If you're a "friend" on Facebook or another social-networking platform, take the time to make comments.

6. If you know a young person who likes to perform, try to attend plays, concerts, or choir performances. Show up. Show up more than once. Say something encouraging afterward.

7. Invite young people to join you in a community service project through a service organization or a faith community. Make it a tradition by inviting kids to participate year after year.

8. Send an e-card or some other online message at least once a month.

9. Start an intergenerational story night in your neighborhood. If you have access to a yard where it's possible, tell tales around a campfire.

10. Invite a young person to start a fun and unusual tradition with you. For example, agree to get together every year on St. Patrick's Day to make green eggs and ham.

11. Bury a time capsule with a child. Fill a container with news clippings

and other mementos to capture today. Return to the spot years later to dig it up together.

12. If you hire a teen for a frequent job such as mowing your lawn or babysitting, use the opportunity to form a lasting connection. Check up to see how things are going personally.

13. Volunteer at a local YMCA or YWCA. Get to know the kids in one of the programs or activities.

14. Play an interactive video game together. Choose one that is likely to last several weeks.

15. Start a neighborhood intergenera-tional softball game once a summer. Make it an annual event.

16. Create a playlist of songs for special occasions. Select upbeat songs for big games or competitions; choose introspective songs for milestones such as the last day of school.

17. Create memorable holiday traditions. For example, hold a dreidel tournament during Hanukkah or a massive outdoor egg hunt during Easter.

18. Ask the kids in your immediate neighborhood to join you in planting one tree every year on Earth Day or Arbor Day.

19. Become a mentor. Contact a local organization or go to mentor.org to learn more. Commit to at least one year of mentoring.

20. Share photos and videos online with young relatives who live far away. Maintain a connection across the distance.

21. Schedule a monthly movie night. Take turns picking films, and always allow plenty of time for discussion afterward.

22. Offer your support to a high school senior who is preparing for college. Help to research scholarships, fill out

paperwork, and go shopping for supplies before the big move.

23. Pass along favorite books you enjoyed when you were a kid. Continue to recommend and discuss age-appropriate books as a child grows older.

24. Recruit a young person to help you in your garden for an entire summer. Get together at least once a week to water the garden, pull weeds, and chat.

25. Make an audio or video recording of yourself reading stories. Send it to a child you don't see very often.

26. Trade lessons with a young person. For example, offer to teach a skill such as baking a pie in exchange for learning from a teen how to open a social-networking account.

27. Look at photo albums together. Nothing brings people together quite like exclamations of "Remember when . . ."

28. Write reference letters for older youth who are applying for jobs or scholarships. Even if teens don't request this, it means a lot to have an adult document the high points in a relationship.

29. Remember to send thoughtful messages on special days such as the first day of summer, Valentine's Day, or the night before a big trip.

30. Pick up the phone and call to say hello. If you get voicemail, take a minute to leave a genuinely thoughtful message.

Stand Up,
Act Up

Be an advocate not only for the young people in your life but also for those in your neighborhood, city, or nation.

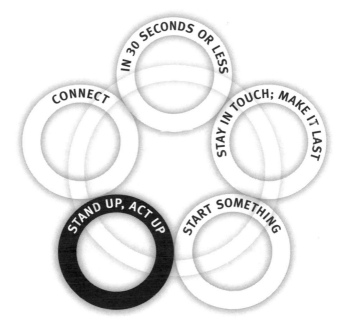

Nothing you do for children is ever wasted. They seem not to notice us, hovering, averting their eyes, and they seldom offer thanks, but what we do for them is never wasted.

GARRISON KEILLOR

You and I have so much potential to love kids. We can do a lot in 30 seconds, or in a long-lasting relationship, or in showing up over and over again. And if we can mobilize most adults to join hands with us, we will make a noticeable difference. We will be halfway home. What do I mean by "halfway"? Let me explain.

There are two major ingredients in the recipe for raising healthy and whole kids. The first is the consistency and intentionality of people, of ordinary people like you and me, being in positive relationships with kids, every chance we get and in moments we choose to create. The second ingredient of the recipe for raising great kids is to guarantee that every one of them has all the resources essential for successful development—things such as strong families and great schools. In agricultural language, these things are the soil in which kids grow.

Too often we plant kids in nutrient-depleted soil—not all kids, but for far too many of them, their families, schools, neighborhoods, and after-school opportunities are broken. Urie Bronfenbrenner, one of the premier developmental psychologists in the world, captured this social dilemma nearly fifteen years ago. There is, he said:

> *A growing chaos in the lives of families, in child care settings, schools, peer groups, youth programs, neighborhoods, workplaces, and other everyday environments in which human beings live their lives. Such chaos, in turn, interrupts and undermines the formation and stability of relationships and activities that are necessary for psychological growth.*[1]

Rather than divvying up the blame or counting the things we lack (money, time, energy), each of us can become an advocate for the experiences all kids deserve.

In addition to building one-on-one relationships with kids, each of us also has voice and influence to stand up and insist that we create rich, life-giving soil for all of our kids. Many people think that it is someone else's job to create the healthy environment all kids need. Not true. Unless you and I raise our voices, this important message may not be heard.

So, in addition to sustained and authentic one-on-one relationships, young people also need us to be advocates who create the conditions that foster growth. These conditions mean access to great schools and great teachers, as well as access to high-quality preschools and out-of-school programs. Kids need health care, access to counselors and social workers, trips to museums and libraries, and people who read to and with them. They need to be involved in volunteer service and opportunities for art, music, drama, and dance. They need to explore the natural world, to be leaders, and to never fear violence or abuse in their families, neighborhoods, and schools.

Although we count on professionals and politicians to ensure these conditions, we know that many of these opportunities are

> **Only an engaged and vocal citizenry can drive positive change for kids.**

fragile in the lives of youth. It is my deep conviction that only an engaged and vocal citizenry can drive change in the direction of creating positive environments for our kids. An active and engaged citizenry—that's you and me. And many of us, when united, can move mountains. Remember the Ethiopian proverb I mentioned earlier in this book? "When spider webs unite, they can tie up a lion."

Is It Good for Kids?

I know people around the country who take a simple question and ask it at every strategic moment: "Is it good for kids?" It's a crucial way to evaluate pending policy questions in local city government deliberations. And someone always needs to raise this question. Take, for example, the decision about where to put a new highway. Cities have to do all kinds of impact assessments before choosing—assessments like, "Does putting it here or there matter for business or the environment?" People rarely pause to ask, "But it is good for kids? Does putting it over there make it harder for kids to access the city park or walk to school? Does it mess up an intact, healthy neighborhood where people know and trust and support each other?" It is not a habit, or a requirement, or a mandate that officials ask these questions. So who will? We have to stand up and act up.

Sometimes we despair when we think of the litany of problems facing children: schools that are falling apart, child abuse and sexual predators, parents who abandon their families, homelessness, teen pregnancy, a lack of access to high-quality health care. In the United States, we have a habit of lamenting these problems, thinking they are beyond our control or are "none of my business." Whose business is it?

When we look at problems through the lens of dark and foreboding images, it is human to feel powerless or to cast blame. I'd like to look through a different lens and ask, "What should we as caring individuals stand for? How could we join hands in common purpose?" This gets me to my favorite topic of all: the shared vision that should connect millions of us in common purpose.

Kids need adults to be their advocates. If we do not step up, who will? Children, of course, have so little voice in matters of policy and investment. They are too young to vote and too often are left out of the deliberations that affect their lives. No wonder we find that, in America, the portion of federal nondefense spending devoted to children's health and welfare shrank 10 percent between 2004 and 2008. Payments to states for foster care dropped 19 percent; investment in the Even Start Family Literacy Program was down 76 percent; education services for homeless children and youth shrank 6 percent; and teacher quality enhancement programs were down 67 percent. Numbers like these are disheartening to say the least.[2]

> **Because kids are too young to vote, they are too often left out of the deliberations that affect their lives.**

If you are over 50, AARP has your back, as do scores of elected officials who know that people over 50 constitute a huge part of the voting public. But who considers each ballot, each vote, in terms of the effects our decisions have on children and teenagers? Who takes these responsibilities personally? What are people doing locally and regionally to take action? Vision of what we want is critical—a vision that ties millions of us in common purpose so that we can be the voice, the noisemakers who ensure that our communities, schools, families, and policies create fertile soil for all of our kids.

Once again, I offer you stories of the things other people are already doing. Some of these individuals are just getting started, and others can already report successes. Their decisions to stand up and act up will make a difference for countless young people in their neighborhoods and even in their nations.

Speaking Up

Delores Jackson is a 54-year-old lifelong resident of a large city in Ohio. Her three kids are grown now. Delores knows how critical art and music were in her kids' development. Over the last 10 years, she has noticed that most of the arts and music programs in the school district have been reduced or eliminated. Not good! she thinks.

> **Only an engaged and vocal citizenry can drive positive change for kids.**

fragile in the lives of youth. It is my deep conviction that only an engaged and vocal citizenry can drive change in the direction of creating positive environments for our kids. An active and engaged citizenry—that's you and me. And many of us, when united, can move mountains. Remember the Ethiopian proverb I mentioned earlier in this book? "When spider webs unite, they can tie up a lion."

Is It Good for Kids?

I know people around the country who take a simple question and ask it at every strategic moment: "Is it good for kids?" It's a crucial way to evaluate pending policy questions in local city government deliberations. And someone always needs to raise this question. Take, for example, the decision about where to put a new highway. Cities have to do all kinds of impact assessments before choosing—assessments like, "Does putting it here or there matter for business or the environment?" People rarely pause to ask, "But it is good for kids? Does putting it over there make it harder for kids to access the city park or walk to school? Does it mess up an intact, healthy neighborhood where people know and trust and support each other?" It is not a habit, or a requirement, or a mandate that officials ask these questions. So who will? We have to stand up and act up.

Sometimes we despair when we think of the litany of problems facing children: schools that are falling apart, child abuse and sexual predators, parents who abandon their families, homelessness, teen pregnancy, a lack of access to high-quality health care. In the United States, we have a habit of lamenting these problems, thinking they are beyond our control or are "none of my business." Whose business is it?

When we look at problems through the lens of dark and foreboding images, it is human to feel powerless or to cast blame. I'd like to look through a different lens and ask, "What should we as caring individuals stand for? How could we join hands in common purpose?" This gets me to my favorite topic of all: the shared vision that should connect millions of us in common purpose.

gave speeches, interviewed candidates, and offered public endorsements for those who best supported the issues that mattered to young people. What started as an individual effort attracted the attention of National Public Radio and other media outlets.[3]

Boys in Trouble

In a world that is generally acknowledged to be controlled by men, we are experiencing something of a paradox that some people call a "boy crisis." Forty-four percent of college graduates today are men. Thirty years ago, that figure was 58 percent. Some may cheer at this shift in numbers and applaud the growth of women in education, but the truth is that too many boys are not doing well in school. Boys are more likely than girls to drop out of school, and three-quarters of the valedictorians in major U.S. cities are girls. If men are dominant in our society, why are they falling further behind in schools?

Dr. Mark Tappan of Colby College in Waterville, Maine, knows about some of the things that boys are going through. "Boys are sent the message that they should be

123

tough and that they don't have to do well in school to be 'real boys.'" The study of boys and masculinity is one of his areas of research, but he also brings the issue close to home as a professor at Colby College. Every week, he and some of his students spend time mentoring boys in the area.

"I divide my class into two-person teams when we go into the middle school. The teams work with groups of half a dozen boys in the school for ten to twelve weeks. Everyone meets for about an hour a week. I specifically have them generate discussion and conversation around the issues of masculinity." The more boys are conscious about the conceptions that society has of what and who boys should be, the more they will be able to deny those ideas and create new images for themselves.

Professor Tappan aims to raise awareness and consciousness about media messages among both his students and the young boys that they mentor in an attempt to counteract some of the messages boys receive about who they should be. This necessarily involves fighting against the "boy code" that says that boys have to be tough in order to be "real boys." In our culture, the toughness factor has been set in opposition to the intelligence factor, giving boys the idea that they cannot be tough and smart at the same time.

"To get at this, here in Central Maine, we are, among other things, helping boys become more critical consumers of the messages they receive from the culture (particularly the media) about what it means to be a 'real boy' or a 'real man' and to resist or challenge those messages. We are trying, in other words, to help boys resist both the pressures and the privileges associated with the boy code. It's not easy, and it's not the whole answer, but it's a start."[4]

For more information on what is going on in the Waterville area with both boys and girls, visit Boys to Men at boystomen .info and Hardy Girls, Healthy Women at hghw.org.

Promoting Teen Voice

One of the best ways to nourish our young people's confidence and skill is to give them opportunities to speak up and influence the things that matter to them. This can include giving them leadership opportunities and/or forums in which adults genuinely listen to their concerns and issues and dreams.

Search Institute has launched, in partnership with the Best Buy Children's Foundation, a national research project to assess the significance of voice among 15-year-olds.[5] The evidence supports two conclusions. First, the frequency of communities tapping youth voice is less than stellar. Second, youth who score high on our Teen Voice Index demonstrate some important benefits that are good for them and our nation. They volunteer more, they are more likely to work up to their ability at school, and they are more likely to develop a sense of purpose and hope for the future.

What does this mean in terms of acting up and standing up? We adults should include teen voice whenever and wherever we can. We can be catalysts who make a point of empowering young people in leadership roles within our communities and organizations.

Taking Responsibility, Taking Action

There is a danger in taking this chapter to heart. If you leave it with the thought, "It's all up to me," then you may get overwhelmed, and your energy will dissipate. If, on the other hand, we identify manageable roles for ourselves, we can set achievable expectations. Remember these things:

- Do what you can.

- Small acts add up.

- Each of us is part of a larger movement. It is not what you or I do, but what *we* do.

- A butterfly fluttering its wings in Peoria can cause a hurricane in Thailand.

- You are not alone.

I didn't get these sentiments from Hallmark cards. They come from the lived experiences of people who care deeply about our society and who, for many years, have been deliberately creating small ripples of change. Believe in your power. Stand up. Act up. Do what you can.

THE **KID-CENTERED**
CONSENSUS

What is it that we can all insist on? I've been asking this question for years in hundreds of cities. From Boston to Biloxi, from liberal audiences to conservative ones, there is a remarkable consensus in our vision. So let's say it and keep it in front of us.

Here's what we agree on:

1. Every kid deserves to be loved.

2. Every kid deserves great schools.

3. Every kid deserves smart, motivated, caring teachers.

4. Every kid deserves a strong family.

5. Every kid deserves to grow up in safe and healthy communities.

6. Every kid deserves to be ready for school.

7. Every kid deserves access to high-quality programs.

8. Every kid deserves access to high-quality health care.

9. Every kid deserves a home with a safe place to sleep, utilities, food, and clothing.

10. Every kid deserves access to high-quality opportunities to explore and express creativity via art, music, drama, and writing.

11. Every kid deserves to be seen, heard, valued, included, and loved by many adults in her or his neighborhoods, families, schools, programs, and communities.

If we were to put this vision to a national vote, the consensus would be overwhelming. There may be disagreements about ways and means and who pays for which parts. For now, let's just hang on to the vision and each ask ourselves what it means to us in our daily lives

Stand Up, Act Up: 30 Ideas for Action

You don't have to give a speech at a rally to show your support for young people. Often the most profound moments of integrity come in the everyday experience of raising your voice to be heard or raising your hand to volunteer.

1. Support the programs through which kids experience art, music, drama, and creative writing. Collect and donate paint, instruments, or costumes.

2. When you see an act of generosity or courage, offer praise and write a letter to the local paper.

3. Look for local events where your high school musicians can entertain.

4. Find ways to involve youth in projects that are not particularly designed for them, such as community gardens or food banks.

5. In every meeting at your school, congregation, or civic organization,

be the one who insists that youth voice and participation are critical.

6. Offer public acknowledgment when young people contribute to community events.

7. Before you vote in elections, find out how kid-friendly each candidate is.

8. Insist that local media focus more on what is right with kids than what is wrong. Make phone calls or write letters to voice your concern when news outlets portray teens negatively.

9. When big decisions are on the table, be the one to ask, "Is it good for kids?"

10. Vote in favor of school bond referenda. Talk to other people about your support for such measures.

11. When you see a parent doing a great job, speak up and say, "I admire how you handled that."

12. If you're a teacher, plan events to get parents involved at school. If you're a parent, show up at those events.

13. If your community event includes a talent show or some other kind of competition, include young people as judges.

14. Send thank-you cards to show your support for school board members who have a compelling vision for all kids in your community.

15. Plan an appreciation event for teachers, program staff, or coaches.

16. Never allow kids' access to camps, programs, lessons, or sports to be limited because they can't afford it. If you can't afford to donate money, help kids raise the money they need to attend.

17. Find out what kinds of early childhood programs exist in your community. Encourage legislators to support such programs. Thank legislators who already have.

18. Stand up for safety in neighbor-hoods. Contact law enforcement officials when you see unsafe conditions for young people.

19. If you attend a church, mosque, or synagogue, participate in activities that reach out and support kids.

20. "Vote with your wallet." Shop at stores that hire young people and support youth groups in the community, and tell the manager why you shop there.

21. Post comments on your local news-paper's website when you read an article about young people.

22. Become a school board member or a community service leader.

23. Offer to be a club sponsor or assistant at your local school.

24. Read up on organizations that support legislation that helps youth. Find out how you can become an activist.

25. Ask other adult friends to join you in a fund-raising campaign for a youth program that matters to you.

26. Empower seniors who live in an assisted living environment. For example, ask for their help in preparing food or decorations for a neighborhood or school event.

27. Speak up when you see a young employee doing a good job. In addition to paying compliments, be sure to tell the manager how impressed you are.

28. When you are at meetings where adults are involved in planning activities for youth, invite a young person to attend with you.

29. Place an ad in your local paper with a compelling message such as, "Have you asked a teenager for advice today?"

30. Don't just drive or walk by and ignore dangerous situations. Stop and get involved when you see bullying, children playing in the street, or other causes for concern.

Start Something

*Create a program, initiative, or other group
opportunity for young people.*

We should be taught not to wait for inspiration to start a thing. Action always generates inspiration. Inspiration seldom generates action.

FRANK TIBOLT

What do you think when you hear the words *start something*? Some people will think simply of beginning, of entering into the first steps of a process. Others will think of rabble-rousers, shaking up expectations, and making waves. In either case, there is an indication of movement, action, and momentum. That's what this chapter is all about.

There is a middle school in Texas that has approximately 1,000 students. Several years ago, the principal decided to find out how well his staff knew the 1,000 students, so he devised the "gold star experiment." In the gymnasium, he gathered all of the adults who worked in that school. All around the walls of the gym, he had taped the names, in big block letters, of each of the 1,000 students—from A to Z, all plain to see. Then he gave gold-star stickers to each of the 100 teachers, administrators, counselors, and support staff. He gave this instruction: "I want you to place a gold star by the name of each student with whom you have a meaningful relationship. By that, I mean you know their passions and dreams, the things that light their fire, and if you saw them out in public, you'd be likely to walk up to them and start a conversation."

The experience in that hot Texas gymnasium was transformative. Here's what the participants learned: about one-quarter of the 1,000 students got lots of gold stars, one-quarter got one or two, and 50 percent got none. None, as in zero, *nada*. Well, this self-discovery changed everything, and the life of that school started to change in a heartbeat. The teachers and other staff willed, at that moment, to become a community of relationships, recognizing that sustained connections with all students are essential for school success. That school is a different place now, and as a by-product, student performance has improved dramatically.

I was telling this story five years ago during a speech at the national board meeting of the YMCA of the USA. I was there, in part, to talk about the YMCA's potential to serve as a national model for creating settings to ensure that every kid is connected to at least one adult who would stay in touch across time. I shared this example to make the point about how easy it is for kids to fall through the cracks and become invisible to us.

When I finished, one of the national board members raised his hand, stood up, and gave this testimonial: "There's no way you could know this, but I live in that city, and my son went to that school. He was entering the eighth grade when that story took place. We had almost lost him in the seventh grade. He was alone, isolated, and depressed. We feared the eighth grade would only make his mood worse. And I can't believe what happened. It's like he walked into a totally different school. Suddenly, he's greeted each day by name, people start conversations with him, and two teachers find out about his interest in music and start to reach out to him. The place turned from an institution into a family overnight. I think it may have saved his life. And I now know how it happened; my kid had no gold stars. Then, in a blink of an eye, he had many."

This whole book has explored what it takes to be a "gold star" for a young person. In this chapter, we take that concept a bit further. How can you be not only a person who provides support but also perhaps the person who takes the initiative to launch a bold new effort—an effort that may even ripple out to touch the lives of many? Whether you are the director of a high-profile national organization like the YMCA or a lone educator with some paper and a bunch of gold stars, you do have the power to start something.

> **How can you be a person who not only provides support but also takes the initiative?**

Where Can I Start?

Many people feel daunted by the idea of being the first person to instigate a new idea or a change in course. Maybe you're not sure what to do, or maybe you don't feel as if you have the time or resources to pull it off. The following examples demonstrate how even small, isolated attempts at new things can yield beautiful results:

YES, BUT *HOW* DO I
START SOMETHING?

Not every person is born a rabble-rouser. You may think "starting something" is beyond your capabilities. If you find yourself feeling stuck, seek help from others. Work through these stages:

1. **Identify a goal.** What is it that you want to accomplish? Do you want to build a skate park? Improve your school's music program? Create an official role for a young person on the city council?

2. **Develop a plan.** What are the steps you'll need to follow? Who needs to be involved? How long do you think it will take?

3. **Garner support.** Talk to the people who can help you make this happen. Contact vendors, legislators, or volunteers to learn how to ensure their involvement.

4. **Seek funding.** Chances are you didn't start this idea with a big budget. Work within your organization or community to discover which money is already available, or plan special events to raise funds.

5. **Make it happen.** Work through the plan with your team. Put your idea into action.

6. **Evaluate.** Thank the people who helped you. Consider what went wrong and what went right. Celebrate the things you achieved.

- Antonio Jackson lived next to an ugly vacant lot in Brooklyn, New York. He imagined turning the lot into a vegetable and flower garden—which he soon did with the help of 15 children and teenagers. The kids come for the beauty of it all, for the sense of accomplishment—and for the connection.

- One family collects children's books from other families they know and delivers boxes of them to day-care centers. They have made this an annual service project, completing their deliveries as part of their family's Easter celebration in the spring.

- A police officer in St. Louis Park, Minnesota, started a summer basketball program for teens who were hanging out with nothing to do. Officers and teens played each other one night a week, and the event drew lots of kids. He sought donations of snacks and prizes. As the police and the teens built relationships, officers noticed that they had better interactions when they went out on calls. Situations that might have been adversarial in the past were positive when kids recognized the officers on duty.

- Ward Clapham was an officer in the Royal Canadian Mounted Police in Richmond, British Columbia. His vision was to help police build constructive connections with kids. He developed the idea of issuing "positive tickets" when kids were caught doing something good. He worked with local businesses to provide additional rewards—ice cream, skating passes, and other prizes—to the youth who received the tickets. Ward and his colleagues have now issued more than 40,000 positive tickets. Youth have developed a much greater trust toward police officers, and—not surprisingly—youth crime fell 41 percent in three years. Other law enforcement officials across North America are now replicating this effective practice.

- A young woman named Jessica Breslawski is serving in the Peace Corps in Kyrgyzstan. She recently held her second annual Asset Development Camp for 40 middle school students in her tiny mountaintop village. The camp experience lasts one week and utilizes Search Institute's model of Developmental Assets to teach leadership skills to the students. Kyrgyzstan is a new country (since 1992), and her students are potential leaders of their government. Jessica was part of an Asset Club while she was a student at Brockport High School in New York. She felt that her participation in asset development was a crucial part of her growth, so she wants to make sure the children in her village are given the same opportunities to grow that she had.

Community Connectors

Sometimes the idea of sustained relationships needs to be ratcheted up to a new level.

My home, Minneapolis, has many of the urban challenges facing New York or Los Angeles. We have neighborhoods in our city where the majority of children are either not ready for school or fail to pass school-based reading and math tests. What we have here—as in many cities—is a need to rethink how kids and families access essential supports and opportunities.

To this end, a network of organizations in Minneapolis has created the Northside Achievement Zone (NAZ). Modeled after the impressive Harlem Children's Zone Geoffrey Canada pioneered in New York City, NAZ has created one particularly powerful innovation for helping children succeed. They are recruiting and training neighbors to be "outreach workers" who work with families to develop long-term school success plans. These NAZ Connectors, as they are called, use the foundation of trusted relationships as the springboard for advocacy, mentoring, and tutoring—bringing needed services right to a family's doorstep. But it all starts with relationships. Once that's established, anything is possible.

To learn more about the work NAZ does, visit northsideachievement.org.

Thinking Big:
Starting a Community Initiative

Hundreds of communities have launched citywide or regional efforts to mobilize schools, families, mentoring programs, after-school programs, and businesses to build Developmental Assets. Sometimes it happens when one or two brave citizens step up and begin the process. Here's one story about how an initiative can take root:

Paradise, California, is a beautiful community situated in the foothills of the Sierra Nevada Mountains. Surrounded by soaring pine trees and the breathtaking Butte Creek Canyon, the small Northern California city appears to be exactly as advertised—paradise. Yet, this idyllic setting could not hide the issues facing the community in the early 2000s. The town was dealing with a drug problem beyond anything it had ever experienced due to widespread illicit use of the prescription pain medi-

FIVE **ACTION** STRATEGIES FOR TRANSFORMING COMMUNITIES

After years of studying and working alongside communities committed to making change happen, Search Institute has identified five action strategies to guide the work residents do in their own towns, cities, or regions. You may find these strategies helpful as you think about "starting something" in your community.

- **Engage adults** from all walks of life to develop sustained, strength-building relationships with children and adolescents, both within families and in neighborhoods.

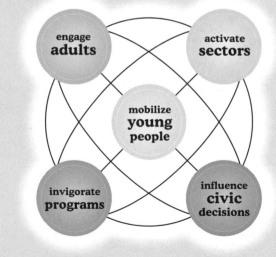

- **Mobilize young people** to have central roles in your efforts. This means listening to their input and including them in decision making.

- **Activate sectors** of the community—such as schools, congregations, businesses, and youth, human service, and health-care organizations—to create a culture that contributes fully to young people's healthy development.

- **Invigorate programs** to become more strength-based and accessible to all children and youth.

- **Influence civic decisions** by encouraging decision makers and opinion leaders to leverage financial, media, and policy resources in support of this positive transformation of communities and society.

As you think about these five action strategies, you will notice that they are not tasks to complete one by one in sequence. Instead, as you strengthen relationships within and between these spheres of influence across the community, you can build a web of interconnected efforts that support one another.

cation OxyContin. Teachers, parents, and community members were at a loss; they had never dealt with anything like this before. The crisis hit its peak when, during the 2003–2004 school year, the 25,000-person community lost four students to overdose and suicide. The town knew something had to be done.

According to Prevention Services Coordinator Jacky Hoiland, "When crisis occurs, there's all this heightened interest in finding out what we have done and what we can do differently . . . there were a lot of people who said we needed to move on to something different as a community." The town was in need of something to rally around and a way to start resolving the serious problems it faced. Then-Superintendent Rick Landess and Hoiland had recently come upon Search Institute's Developmental Assets and decided to use this approach to engage the community with its troubled youth.

The planning event, as Hoiland explains, was a chance for the community to come together and really dig deeply into resolving its problems by learning the asset approach and partnering with its kids. Hoiland had hoped to gather 30 people for the initial workshop; however, on May 15, 2004, 85 individuals between the ages of 14 and 70 came together to face the life-and-death issues surrounding the community and build a plan for the future of Paradise. "It was one very long, hard, and meaningful day," said Hoiland.

The people of Paradise worked together to move beyond their pain and find ways adults and youth could work together to create a better Paradise. The youth at the event were astounded by the outpouring of support they felt and their ability to speak freely and honestly with adults. Landess recalls one high school junior's reflection at the end of the event: "If kids in this town knew how many adults care about them, we wouldn't be doing all the things we're doing."

Following the training event, the citizens of Paradise renewed their commitment to asset building by creating new organizations and integrating the asset approach into existing programs. The community formed a task force called Project Vision, which partners with other community groups to build assets. The task force has held community forums of youth-serving organizations and given out mini-grants for youth projects in the community. It also created a local youth council. At the time of its inception, the council was a formal liaison with the town council, but since 2004, it has become an all-youth-led initiative where the young people involved decide what projects to tackle and how to reach their goals. The police department and Boys and Girls Clubs have also become asset builders by giving youth avenues to get involved in their community.

All of this began with a couple of people struggling to respond to tragedy,

> **The youth at the event were astounded by the outpouring of support they felt and their ability to speak freely and honestly with adults.**

but now it has become a community-wide transformation. "Our efforts continue to see where we can move youth into positions where they feel like they have some meaningful part to play," said Hoiland.[1]

Starting a community initiative can help you not only to shape relationships between adults and youth but also to change the collective experience of living together in a neighborhood, town, or city. To learn more about Healthy Communities • Healthy Youth initiatives, visit search-institute .org/hc-hy.

Start Something: 30 Ideas for Action

You started this book with 30-second interactions, and look how far you've come! What have you learned about your capacity to make a difference? Which "something" will you start?

1. Ask a young person, "If there's one thing you could change about your school, what would it be?" Help her or him act on the idea.

2. Start a book drive for a day-care center.

3. If your school district is cutting back on arts, music, or drama, raise your voice in protest. Be vocal at school board meetings and help out with fund-raising.

4. Get mad at policies, programs, and people that damage kids. Speak up and say what kind of changes you want to see.

5. Plan community intergenerational gatherings where adults and kids interact. Street dances, game nights, and parades are all good opportunities to connect.

6. Launch a community education course for teens. Teach life skills such as cooking or filling out job applications.

7. If you own a business or lead an organization, hire a group of teens to conduct a "walk-through." Ask

them to tell you what you can do to make your setting more welcoming to young people.

8. Start a "Spark Club" where kids can talk about the things they are passionate about.

9. In lieu of birthday presents for yourself, ask friends and family to give you kids' books, prom dresses, or instruments you can donate to a local school or program.

10. Start a book club for adults who care about kids. Read books about parenting, education, and other topics that influence young people.

11. Start a youth group in your neighborhood recreational center or faith community.

12. Supply all of the materials for a lemonade stand. Put your young neighbors in charge, and challenge them to donate half of their earnings to a good cause.

13. Put an ad in the newspaper offering to be a tutor or to teach lessons in something.

14. Build a website to feature a young person's artwork.

15. Schedule training in your school or community to improve adults' ability to connect with kids.

16. Invite new neighbors to go on a walking tour. Ask at least one teenager to accompany you as a guide.

17. If you are a parent, ask your child and her or his friends to select a service project. Schedule an event where they can all volunteer together.

18. Make T-shirts for all the parents of your school's athletes; feature messages about sportsmanship and positive communication.

19. Create a fan page or application on a social-networking site for high school teams and activities (basketball, drama club, etc.).

20. If you participate in a church, mosque, or synagogue, create a "Phone-a-Friend" list for the kids in your congregation. Let families know the names and numbers of adults who are available if kids need to talk.

21. Find a coffee club or another local business that will sponsor "open mic" nights for young musicians or poets.

22. Volunteer to coordinate events at school. Identify special occasions that might deserve more attention, such as the last day of a semester or the math team's first competition.

23. Write a blog that tells stories about inspiring young people.

24. Put students in charge of lesson plans for a full week.

25. Schedule a job fair at a local school.

26. If your community doesn't have a 4-H club or a Boy Scout or Girl Scout troop, learn how to start one.

27. If you teach a young person a skill, host an event to showcase it. One 15-year-old had a mentor who gave her sewing lessons every week from grade 4 to grade 7. As their lessons came to a close, the mentor planned a public fashion show where her mentee modeled her creations.

28. Start a cheering squad for a school activity that usually doesn't get much attention. Create chants and locker decorations for Knowledge Bowl or one of the school's bands.

29. Ask your employer to create a scholarship for a local high school.

30. Run for public office and use your position to vote for issues that affect children and teens.

EPILOGUE: 75 MILLION GEMS

There are 75 million children in the United States. Each is a gem, but many remain invisible—waiting to be seen and discovered. Waiting to shine and add beauty to our world.

Sometimes even the most optimistic adults find themselves looking at parenting, teaching, or other youth work as a daily burden— a series of chores to be completed. We mean well, but we get tired. We forget to pay attention. We overlook the gems in our midst.

What might happen if we saw ourselves as jewelers?

As you take the ideas from this book and put them into action, look around you to spot the glimmers of possibility.

Although a good jeweler can see the flaws and imperfections, you can also bring out the potential in each gem you discover. Showcase the warmth or strength of each one. Place them in settings that make them gleam. Pick them up and polish them when they feel scuffed, scratched, or damaged.

More than anything, this book is about discovering possibilities. You already care. You have already been making efforts, big and small, to be a positive influence in someone's world. But I hope this book has given you keener senses. Now you have five new ways to think about connecting with kids. You have 150 ideas for making it happen. The trick is to keep your eye out, to notice each glistening opportunity to make a difference in a young life.

Whether you take 30 seconds to acknowledge a young person or spend a lifetime actively engaging with kids, know that there are 75 million gems waiting to be discovered. And your efforts are making the world brighter.

For these are all our children,

and we shall profit by, or pay for,

what they become.

JAMES BALDWIN

NOTES

A Call to Action

1. This international study of adolescence is supported by the John Templeton Foundation. Visit spiritualdevelopment center.org to learn more.

2. For a detailed summary of the research on Developmental Assets, see Benson, P. L. 2006. *All kids are our kids: What communities must do to raise caring and responsible children and adolescents.* San Francisco: Jossey-Bass.

3. For a review of the literature on nonparent adult support for youth, see Scales, P. C., and J. L. Gibbons. 1996. Extended family members and unrelated adults in the lives of young adolescents: A research agenda. *Journal of Early Adolescence,* 16 (4): 365–389.

4. Hersch, P. 1998. *A tribe apart: A journey into the heart of American adolescence,* 14. New York: Ballantine.

5. Rhodes, J. E. 2002. *Older and wiser: Risks and rewards in youth mentoring.* Cambridge: Harvard University Press.

6. Story adapted from Benson, P. 2006. *All kids are our kids: What communities must do to raise caring and responsible children and adolescents,* 227. San Francisco: Jossey-Bass.

In 30 Seconds or Less

1. Story adapted from Fisher, D. 2004. *Just when I needed you: True stories of adults who made a difference in the lives of young people,* 20–23. Minneapolis: Search Institute.

2. Story adapted from Fisher, D. 2004. *Just when I needed you: True stories of adults who made a difference in the lives of young people,* 101–103. Minneapolis: Search Institute.

3. The first study, conducted in 2000 by the Gallup Organization, consisted of a nationally representative telephone survey of 1,425 American adults and in-depth interviews with a subset of 100 survey participants. Findings are reported in Scales, P. C., with P. L. Benson, M. Mannes, E. C. Roehlkepartain, N. R. Hintz, and T. K. Sullivan. 2003. *Other people's kids: Social expectations and American adults' involvement with children and adolescents.* New York: Kluwer Academic/Plenum. The second

study, conducted in 2002, involved Gallup telephone surveys of 1,425 adults and 614 adolescents, ages 12 to 17. See Scales, P. C., P. L. Benson, and M. Mannes. 2002. *Grading grown-ups 2002: How do American kids and adults relate? A national study.* Minneapolis: Search Institute.

Connect

1. Milliken, B. 2007. *The last dropout: Stop the epidemic!* 9–10. Carlsbad, California: Hay House, Inc.

2. Benson, P. 1990. Help-seeking for alcohol and drug problems: To whom do adolescents turn? *Journal of Adolescent Chemical Dependency* 1: 83–94.

3. Scales, P. C. Building your tennis players' Developmental Assets and success for life. *ADDvantage* magazine. Article expected to appear in 2010. *ADDvantage* magazine is the official publication of the U.S. Professional Tennis Association.

4. For more on thriving and the idea of sparks, see Benson, P. L. 2008. *Sparks: How parents can help ignite the hidden strengths of teenagers.* San Francisco: Jossey-Bass. See also Benson, P. L., and P. C. Scales. 2009. The definition and measurement of thriving in adolescence. *Journal of Positive Psychology* 4(1): 85–104.

Stay in Touch; Make It Last

1. Collins, P. H. 1987. The meaning of motherhood in black culture and black mother/daughter relationships. *Sage: A Scholarly Journal on Black Women* 4: 3–10.

2. Brendtro, L., and M. Brokenleg. 2001. The circles of courage: Children as sacred beings. In L. Lantieri, ed. *Schools with spirit: Nurturing the inner lives of children and teachers*, 39–52. Boston: Beacon Press.

3. From the Committee on Increasing High School Students' Engagement and Motivation to Learn (2003). The National Research Council (p. 6).

4. Story adapted from Gemelke, T. 2005. *Stay close: 40 clever ways to connect with kids when you're apart*, 41–42. Minneapolis: Search Institute.

5. Story adapted from Fisher, D. 2004. *Just when I needed you: True stories of adults who made a difference in the lives of young people*, 58–60. Minneapolis: Search Institute.

Stand Up, Act Up

1. Bronfenbrenner, U., and P. Morris. 1998. The ecology of developmental processes. In *Handbook of child psychology: Vol. 1. Theoretical models of human development*, 5th ed., ed. W. Damon and R. M. Lerner, 993–1028. New York: Wiley.

2. First Focus, *First Focus children's budget 2008* (Washington, D.C., 2008). For more information about related trends in funding, visit FirstFocus.net.

3. Brady, J. (2004) "The Kids Campaign: Colorado 10-year-old runs her own political action committee." Featured on National Public Radio on July 16, 2004. Read the story at npr.org.

4. Adapted from "Working with boys in Maine," an article originally published in the September 2007 issue of Search Institute's online newsletter, *The Asset Champion*.

5. Scales, P. C., E. C. Roehlkepartain, and P. L. Benson. 2010. *Teen voice 2010: Relationships that matter to America's teens.* This report, developed with the Best Buy Children's Foundation, can be accessed at at15.com.

Start Something

1. Adapted from "From crisis to community: Paradise, California," an article originally published in the September 2009 issue of Search Institute's online newsletter, *The Asset Champion*.

What Are Developmental Assets?

The Developmental Assets are a set of positive qualities, skills, experiences, and opportunities that are critical to foster during adolescent years, helping youth to become caring, reliable adults. Spread across eight broad areas of human development, these assets paint a picture of the positive things all young people need to grow up healthy and responsible. The first four asset categories focus on external structures, relationships, and activities that create a positive environment for young people:

Support
Young people need to be surrounded by adults and peers who love, care for, appreciate, and accept them. They need to know that they belong and that they are not alone.

Empowerment

Young people need to feel valued and valuable. This happens when youth feel safe, when they believe that they are liked and respected, and when they contribute to their families and communities.

Boundaries and Expectations

Young people need the positive influence of peers and adults who encourage them to be and do their best. Youth also need clear rules about appropriate behavior and consistent, reasonable consequences for breaking those rules.

Constructive Use of Time

Young people need opportunities—outside of school—to learn and develop new skills and interests and to spend enjoyable time interacting with other youth and adults.

The next four categories reflect internal values, skills, and beliefs that young people also need to develop in order to fully engage with and function in the world around them:

Commitment to Learning

Young people need a variety of learning experiences, including the desire for academic success, a sense of the lasting importance of learning, and a belief in their own abilities.

Positive Values
Young people need to develop strong guiding values or principles, including caring about others, having high standards for personal character, and believing in protecting their own well-being.

Social Competencies
Young people need to develop the skills to interact effectively with others, to make difficult decisions and choices, and to cope with new situations.

Positive Identity
Young people need to believe in their own self-worth, to feel that they have control over the things that happen to them, and to have a sense of purpose in life as well as a positive view of the future.

See the full list of Developmental Assets on the following pages.

40 Developmental Assets for Adolescents (Ages 12–18)

Search Institute has identified the following "building blocks" of healthy development that help young people grow up healthy, caring, and responsible.

EXTERNAL ASSETS

Support

1. *Family Support*—Family life provides high levels of love and support.

2. *Positive Family Communication*—Young person and her or his parent(s) communicate positively, and young person is willing to seek advice and counsel from parent(s).

3. *Other Adult Relationships*—Young person receives support from three or more nonparent adults.

4. *Caring Neighborhood*—Young person experiences caring neighbors.

5. *Caring School Climate*—School provides a caring, encouraging environment.

6. *Parent Involvement in Schooling*—Parent(s) are actively involved in helping young person succeed in school.

Empowerment

7. *Community Values Youth*—Young person perceives that adults in the community value youth.

8. *Youth as Resources*—Young people are given useful roles in the community.

9. *Service to Others*—Young person serves in the community one hour or more per week.

10. *Safety*—Young person feels safe at home, at school, and in the neighborhood.

Boundaries and Expectations

11. *Family Boundaries*—Family has clear rules and consequences and monitors the young person's whereabouts.

12. *School Boundaries*—School provides clear rules and consequences.

13. *Neighborhood Boundaries*—Neighbors take responsibility for monitoring young people's behavior.

14. *Adult Role Models*—Parent(s) and other adults model positive, responsible behavior.

15. *Positive Peer Influence*—Young person's best friends model responsible behavior.

16. *High Expectations*—Both parent(s) and teachers encourage the young person to do well.

Constructive Use of Time

17. *Creative Activities*—Young person spends three or more hours per week in lessons or practice in music, theater, or other arts.

18. *Youth Programs*—Young person spends three or more hours per week in sports, clubs, or organizations at school and/or in the community.

19. *Religious Community*—Young person spends one or more hours per week in activities in a religious institution.

20. *Time at Home*—Young person is out with friends "with nothing special to do" two or fewer nights per week.

INTERNAL ASSETS

Commitment to Learning

21. *Achievement Motivation*—Young person is motivated to do well in school.

22. *School Engagement*—Young person is actively engaged in learning.

23. *Homework*—Young person reports doing at least one hour of homework every school day.

24. *Bonding to School*—Young person cares about her or his school.

25. *Reading for Pleasure*—Young person reads for pleasure three or more hours per week.

Positive Values

26. *Caring*—Young person places high value on helping other people.

27. *Equality and Social Justice*—Young person places high value on promoting equality and reducing hunger and poverty.

28. *Integrity*—Young person acts on convictions and stands up for her or his beliefs.

29. *Honesty*—Young person "tells the truth even when it is not easy."

30. *Responsibility*—Young person accepts and takes personal responsibility.

31. *Restraint*—Young person believes it is important not to be sexually active or to use alcohol or other drugs.

Social Competencies

32. *Planning and Decision Making*—Young person knows how to plan ahead and make choices.

33. *Interpersonal Competence*—Young person has empathy, sensitivity, and friendship skills.

34. *Cultural Competence*—Young person has knowledge of and comfort with people of different cultural/racial/ethnic backgrounds.

35. *Resistance Skills*—Young person can resist negative peer pressure and dangerous situations.

36. *Peaceful Conflict Resolution*—Young person seeks to resolve conflict nonviolently.

Positive Identity

37. *Personal Power*—Young person feels he or she has control over "things that happen to me."

38. *Self-Esteem*—Young person reports having a high self-esteem.

39. *Sense of Purpose*—Young person reports that "my life has a purpose."

40. *Positive View of Personal Future*—Young person is optimistic about her or his personal future.

The Power of Assets

On one level, the 40 Developmental Assets represent common wisdom about the kinds of positive experiences and characteristics that young people need and deserve. But their value extends further. Surveys of more than 2 million young people in grades 6–12 have shown that assets are powerful influences on adolescent behavior. (The following numbers reflect 2003 data from 148,189 young people in 202 communities.) Regardless of the gender, ethnic heritage, economic situation, or geographic location of the youth surveyed, these assets promote positive behaviors and attitudes and help protect young people from many different problem behaviors.

| 0–10 | 11–20 | 21–30 | 31–40 |
| ASSETS | ASSETS | ASSETS | ASSETS |

Figure 1: Promoting Positive Behaviors and Attitudes

Search Institute research shows that the more assets students report having, the more likely they also are to report the following patterns of thriving behavior:

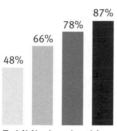

Exhibits Leadership
Has been a leader of an organization or group in the past 12 months.

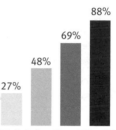

Maintains Good Health
Takes good care of body (such as eating foods that are healthy and exercising regularly).

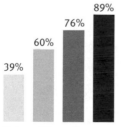

Values Diversity
Thinks it is important to get to know people of other racial/ethnic groups.

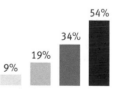

Succeeds in School
Gets mostly As on report card (an admittedly high standard).

Figure 2: Protecting Youth from High-Risk Behaviors

Assets not only promote positive behaviors—
they also protect young people. The more assets
a young person reports having, the less likely
she is to make harmful or unhealthy choices.
(Note that these definitions are set rather high,
suggesting ongoing problems rather than experi-
mentation.)

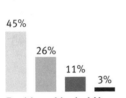

45%

26%

11%

3%

Problem Alcohol Use
Has used alcohol three or
more times in the past 30
days or got drunk once or
more in the past two weeks.

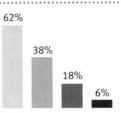

62%

38%

18%

6%

Violence
Has engaged in three or
more acts of fighting,
hitting, injuring a person,
carrying a weapon, or
threatening physical harm
in the past 12 months.

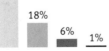

38%

18%

6%

1%

Illicit Drug Use
Used illicit drugs (mari-
juana, cocaine, LSD, PCP
or angel dust, heroin, or
amphetamines) three or
more times in the past 12
months.

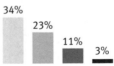

34%

23%

11%

3%

Sexual Activity
Has had sexual inter-
course three or more
times in lifetime.

178

APPENDIX B
What Are Sparks?

It Begins with a Spark

A spark is a special quality, skill, or interest that lights us up and that we are passionate about. A spark comes from inside of us, and when we express it, it gives us joy and energy. It's our very essence, the thing about us that is good, beautiful, and useful to the world.

Each of us—young or old or in between—has (or can have) at least one spark. A few people seem to know their spark from an early age, but for most of us, our spark is revealed or discovered over time, through many opportunities and experiences, and we often need caring adults to point them out as we grow from ages 10 to 20.

Sparks come in many forms. Search Institute's national studies of 12- to 17-year-olds provide many examples: leading a group, playing an instrument, restoring old cars, dancing, advocating for animal rights, helping people who are injured or abused, writing, making movies, learning, inventing, acting. Others surveyed in the research were still searching, trying things, and volunteering as they looked to discover a spark. Clearly, for all of us, the possibilities are wide open!

Why Do Sparks Matter?

When young people know and develop a spark, with the support of several adults, they present a strong picture of health and well-being. Our new research shows that they:

- Have higher grades in school
- Have better school attendance
- Are more likely to be socially competent
- Are more likely to be physically healthy
- Are more likely to volunteer to help other people
- Are more likely to care about the environment
- Are more likely to have a sense of purpose
- Are less likely to experience depression
- Are less likely to engage in acts of violence

But in our national surveys, we found that while 65 percent know their spark, only about 37 percent of young people could both name a spark and claim the adult support they need to develop it. Our work is cut out for us: we've got to start and nurture caring, supportive relationships with young people so we can help them find and pursue their sparks.

What Can Adults Do to Nurture Sparks?

People often view the problems young people have with drugs, alcohol, pregnancy, and dropping out of school as social ills that need fixing. Let's try viewing them as what happens when kids are disconnected from their sparks and lack relationships with caring, responsible adults who could help them. From this point of view, any adult helping a young person find and nurture her or his spark is helping not only that young person but also potentially the whole community.

So what will we do differently? We can start small and start personally with sparks, and then the bigger change for young people's lives will grow out of the changes we make in how we interact with them. Because when we, as adults, change our behavior toward young people, when we change how we listen and how we talk, we change the relationships between us. When we begin not by telling them what they should do but by asking them who they are and what they love to do, our message to young people is this: you are unique, you are valuable just the way you are, and I'm interested in knowing the real you. That is a strong opening for a healthy new relationship, and a good, deepening direction for an existing relationship.

In fact, that's the beginning of everything good that we want to happen for our children and youth. Because it is through good relationships that young people:

- Get support and encouragement;

- Learn values and know their identity is affirmed;

- Become courageous about trying new things;

- Learn to persevere through difficulties; and

- Come to have all the resources that not only help them survive but lead them toward thriving.

Whether you take the small step of talking with your own child about sparks, or you incorporate the idea of sparks into your workplace or classroom, or you go further and begin asset building as well, you'll be making a positive difference in young people's lives, and in your community. And, by the way, you will also bring untold joy and fulfillment into your own life.

For further information, see P. L. Benson (2008), *Sparks: How Parents Can Help Ignite the Hidden Strengths of Teenagers.* San Francisco:

Jossey-Bass. Visit ignitesparks.org and search institute.org to discover the tools, books, trainings, surveys, and other resources that can help you nurture young people's sparks and build assets for and with them. The concepts of thriving and sparks owe much to the generous support of the Thrive Foundation for Youth.

DISCUSSION GUIDE:
QUESTIONS TO GET GROUPS THINKING,
TALKING, AND ACTING

Individual action is crucial, but you may also find it helpful to discuss the content of this book in groups. Whether you are meeting in parenting classes, professional development sessions, or less formal settings such as congregations or neighborhood groups, take time to reflect together and share ideas about reaching out to kids.

Questions for Parents

1. Think back over the last week. What were some of the 30-second opportunities you took to connect with your child? What were some of the 30-second opportunities you missed?

2. Who is one adult your child trusts? How might you foster a stronger relationship between your child and that adult? What specific activity could you schedule?

3. Who are the people in your life who support you as a parent? What kinds of things do they do to support you?

4. Are you getting as much support as you need as a parent? Who do you call when you need advice?

5. Think about your child's friends. How do you make them feel welcome in your home? What kinds of conversations do you have with them?

6. How well do you and your neighbors know each other? How do adults in your neighborhood interact with kids?

7. Do you know what your child's "spark" is? How do you nurture the things your child is passionate about?

8. How do you thank the people who make a difference in your child's life?

Questions for Teachers

1. How do you find time to build relationships with students? What are some of the 30-second opportunities in your average day?

2. How do you balance the dynamics of managing a whole classroom with the needs of individual students?

3. What are some things you've done to connect with students? How do you offer one-on-one support without playing favorites?

4. How often do you see or talk to former students?

5. What makes it hard to form relationships with students? What would make it easier?

6. Have you ever changed a student's life? How can you tell if you're having an impact?

7. Do you know what your students' "sparks" are? How do you nurture the things your students are passionate about?

Questions for Mentors

1. What made you decide to become a mentor? What were your fears? What were your hopes?

2. Describe a moment when you felt as if you could not connect with your mentee. What would have made it easier?

3. Think about a time when you and your mentee seemed to connect. What seemed to make it work?

4. Do you know what your mentee's "spark" is? How do you nurture the things your mentee is passionate about?

5. How well do you know your mentee's family? How might you get to know them better?

6. What kinds of activities and conversations help you feel closer in your mentoring relationship rather than "just hanging out"?

7. What advice would you give to other people who are just starting out as mentors?

Questions for Adult Friends

Not every caring adult in a child's life plays a formal role. Even if you don't work within a school or youth-serving program, you may have lots of opportunities to connect with kids in your neighborhood, faith community, or workplace.

1. Where do you most frequently spend time with children and teenagers? How do you greet them or interact with them?

2. What kinds of questions do you ask to start conversations with kids? How do you get beyond simply asking how school is going?

3. What kind of relationship do you have with your friends' kids? How might you be more involved in their lives?

4. What kinds of things do you do to make kids feel valued in your neighborhood?

5. Think of a local business where teenagers are employed. What kinds of compliments could you give them when they do a good job? How might you offer advice when they are struggling?

6. How might you reassure parents that they can trust you?

ACKNOWLEDGMENTS

Writing a book, at least for me, is always a team effort. There are three circles of support that have made this one possible. The first circle is the incredible staff at Search Institute. My colleagues and friends here, supplemented by the 20 outstanding trainers and consultants who make up Vision Training Associates, provided valuable insight, practical wisdom, and intellectual grounding for the ideas in *Parent, Teacher, Mentor, Friend.* They have done this, for sure, during the year of manuscript preparation. As importantly, they have been nurturing my thinking for many years. All of us are really one organism, one entity, working in solidarity to imagine how to mobilize our nation's people to provide all of the "nutrients" our kids need to succeed. I am deeply grateful to each and every person who calls Search Institute home base. I am particularly thankful for the wonderful support provided by Tenessa Gemelke, Search Institute's publishing manager, who held my hand through the writing process, kept me on target, and edited the work with both firmness and grace. I am grateful to Mary Ellen Buscher for creatively overseeing the design of the book, and to Melody St. Marie who so expertly watches over my work and writing.

The second circle of support is provided by literally thousands of advocates for kids who are out in America's cities and towns, working in schools, programs, and agencies to equip people to build vibrant and life-changing relationships with our nation's young. This network of asset champions is the lifeblood for our work. They are kindred spirits who help all of us step up to the plate. I give my thanks to all of these friends and allies, and especially to the many who provided story ideas for this book.

At the third level are the decision makers and actors who ensure Search Institute's strength and success. I send my thanks to each member of the Search Institute board of directors. This great team of leaders gave me the space and time to create this work. Though our work is supported by dozens of foundations and corporations, I give a shout-out here to the Manuel D. and Rhoda Mayerson Foundation, and particularly to Neal and Donna Mayerson, for believing in me and us, and to the Thrive Foundation for Youth for its sustained support of our work on sparks and thriving.

At the very center of my support system is my family. To Tunie, my extraordinary life partner, and to Liv and Kai, my creative and inspiring kids, I give my enduring thanks for believing in me. And then there are Ryder and Truman, my grandchildren and the source for many of my best moments in life. I love who you are and what you are becoming.

Peter L. Benson
Minneapolis, Minnesota
August 2010

ABOUT THE AUTHOR

Peter L. Benson, Ph.D., is president and CEO of Minneapolis-based Search Institute and is one of the world's leading authorities on positive human development. He weaves together rigorous scholarship with a commitment to influencing society to be more attentive to children and adolescents. He is a widely sought speaker, writer, and consultant for major national and international events and policy initiatives. He is the author of 15 books, including *What Kids Need to Succeed, All Kids Are Our Kids,* and *Sparks: How Parents Can Help Ignite the Hidden Strengths of Teenagers.*

Dr. Benson holds an M.A. and a Ph.D. in experimental social psychology, with a concentration in child development, from the University of Denver. His international reputation in human development emerged in the 1990s through his innovative, research-based framework of Developmental Assets, the most widely recognized approach to positive youth development in the United States and, increasingly, around the world. His vision, research, and public voice have inspired a sea change in research, practice, and policy.

Dr. Benson is married to Tunie Munson-Benson, a nationally recognized expert in children's literature and literacy. They have two children, Liv and Kai, and two grandsons, Ryder and Truman.

ABOUT SEARCH INSTITUTE PRESS

Search Institute Press is a division of Search Institute, a nonprofit organization that offers leadership, knowledge, and resources to promote positive youth development. Our mission at Search Institute Press is to provide practical and hope-filled resources to help create a world in which all young people thrive. Our products are based in research, and the 40 Developmental Assets—qualities, experiences, and relationships youth need to succeed—are a central focus of our resources.